DZELARHONS

Myths of the Northwest Coast

ANNE CAMERON

DZELARHONS

MYTHS OF THE NORTHWEST COAST

HARBOUR PUBLISHING
MADEIRA PARK   1986

Published by Harbour Publishing Co. Ltd., P.O. Box 219,
Madeira Park, BC, Canada. All rights reserved.

Cover painting, *Rainbow*, by Art Thompson

Printed and bound in Canada

Canadian Cataloguing in Publication Data

Cameron, Anne, 1938—
  Dzelarhons

  ISBN 0-920080-89-8

  1. Indians of North America—British Columbia—
Vancouver Island—Fiction.   I. Title.
PS8555.A44D94 1986   C813'.54   C86-091503-4
PR9199.3.C34D94 1986

For *Alex*
Erin
Pierre
Marianne
Tara

and especially Eleanor

Other books by Anne Cameron

CONTENTS

FOREWORD

When I was eight or nine—or maybe ten or eleven—I don't remember for sure now, Klopinum would share her stories with me. My mom was working as an aide in the white hospital at the top of the hill where black-haired kids with eyes like sad holes burned in wool blankets stared through windows at the rolling fields their TB lungs would not allow them to run in, or to jump or yell or chase or ride bikes or do any of the things kids were intended by creation to do.

"You be good now," my mom would say and off she'd go, leaving her own kids at home, walking a mile or so to the job that provided the money there was no other way to get, the money that bought the food that kept us healthy. Sometimes, especially when she was on afternoon shift, I'd half waken, and she'd be standing by my bed looking down at me, her eyes glistening damply in the one A.M. moontinted darkness. She had a real thing about those forms they sent home from school; she'd always sign, and they'd jab us in the arm with all this stuff she said would keep us from getting sick. Didn't matter if it was smallpox, typhoid, diphtheria, she didn't even look at the form, she signed and we got stuck in the arm. But we didn't get the TB or anything else, except one summer I got undulant fever from cow's milk. She'd tell us, "Stop complaining, the kids where I work would give anything to be able to do what you do." Not much we could say in answer to that, just roll up the sleeve and get jabbed again, and put a good face on it. Life could be worse and for a lot of people it is.

Anyway, she'd go off to work, and I'd feed the few scraggly hens I had in a coop under the steps against the front of the house, safe from neighbours' dogs and hungry 'coons. One of my first abortive attempts at capitalism, probably the reason I sympathize with wheat farmers today. Fill their water, gather the occasional egg, take it in the house and wash off the chickenshit, feathers, mud, and who knows what all, clean the sink, wash the dishes, clean the sink again, and the day was mine.

Get the red CCM from where it was leaning against the outside wall, start running with it, pushing it alongside, then, when everything felt right, jump up on the seat, as close as I could get to the running starts the cowboys took in the Saturday matinees. Even then I wondered how often they fell off before they learned how.

Down the camp road to Fifth Street, then straight down Fifth, all the way to where it turned into Pine. Why two names for one street? Nobody ever explained. To the highway, turn left, then turn right,

down, over the tracks to the reserve, past the big
building, and you could see the church off to your
right, standing in a field of grass, the whitepainted
walls and big cross on the black roof sharp in the
summer holiday sun. Down the street that ran along
the beach; it had no name then, God knows if it has
one now.

Dogs, dogs, dogs. Everywhere. With and without
puppies tagging along behind. Some friendly, some
waiting for the chance to rip your flesh, they'd run
and boil around in the soft dusty road, yapping and
barking, almost upsetting the bike, until someone
would holler, and then the whole mad lot would
chase off in search of some other entertainment.
Kids yelled, or waved, or grinned, or ignored me.
Adults sat on the steps or porches, the men in dark
pants and undershirts, the women in cotton dresses,
the old women with kerchiefs over their heads, tied
at the back of their necks, white hair straying and
wisping from under the blue or green cloth. The
kids, like me, in old clothes, "play clothes" we called
them to distinguish them from "school clothes"
which had to be kept clean.

The open doors gaped darkly, even in broad
daylight, windows shoved up and held open with a
length of kindling stick, no screens in evidence,
mosquitoes and flies probably waiting inside, but
only the toddlers seemed to have any bites. Nobody
ever seemed in a rush, nobody ever seemed to be out
of sorts. Oh, once in a while you'd see some guy
draped over a fencepost or on his knees by a ditch
puking his guts out drunk, and sometimes there'd be
a couple of guys sprawled near the steps they hadn't
been able to manoeuvre, sleeping it off in the heat,
but none of the sober ones seemed to pay any

11

attention to it. A lot of the kids had marks like the kind I wore a lot, those hot red blotches where the old man's hand connected with a good one, or those fire red strips where the belt cracked sharply against your skin. But in that town at that time all the kids were marked up like that, it was how they socialized you, making the boys into men and the girls into women, fitting them for the coal mines or the kitchen, the logging slopes or the bedroom.

Where the road, such as it was, ended, the path started. Unless you knew where you were going, you'd think the houses stopped at the place where the road stopped, but two minutes down the path, shoving the CCM through grass and tangleberry and ground blackberry that committed mayhem on your bare ankles, was Klopinum's house. Set all by itself. Small, tidy, if it had ever been painted the salt air and wind had fixed that; the boards were silver gray, grainy where the fine sand had rubbed the soft part and left the harder wood exposed in dry pencil-like strips. Her dog would come down the walk, moving oddly, almost half-curled in a sort of slinky-skulk, and for the first few visits, I was sure the dog was going to bite me. I could see teeth, see its lips wrinkled back in what I was sure was a vicious wolf-like snarl, and then I realized the dog was smiling. I'd never seen a dog smile before in my life, was afraid to mention it in case everyone laughed at me and said I was either making up stories again, or so dumb I didn't know a snarl from a grin. Sort of pale honeybrown splotches on a mostly white body, smiling and whipping its tail in circles. Klopinum insisted it was a border collie, but I never saw one like it before or since, although border collies are known to smile that way.

I suppose that dog had a name, but I can't remember what it was.

For years I didn't even know Klopinum's name; if she'd ever told me, I had forgotten. I just called her "Auntie." If any other Auntie came to visit while I was there, Klopinum would tell her my name and add, "her momma works at our hospital," and the other Auntie would look at me as if I had just been forgiven something. Twenty-five years later, in Alert Bay, on hearing my name, someone, a fisherman who sang country and western, asked "where you from?", and I said, "Nanaimo." He asked if I was related to the woman with the same name who had worked in the Indian hospital. I said, "She's my mom," and right then and there I had to go to his house, meet his wife, see his kids, hold the baby, and out came the photo album. There was my mom, magically young again, standing by a white painted metal crib, her arm around a boy of five or six, both of them smiling, and another picture, the same boy in pajamas, sitting grinning from ear to ear at a small table, and on the table a stack of presents, a birthday cake, some funny paper hats. And my mom again, laughing, ready to help him blow out his candles. "She was like my own mom when I didn't have one," he said, and his wife told me to stay for supper. Before the meal was over there were brothers and sisters, an uncle and a few aunts, smiling, telling me to please tell my mom thank you for being so nice to Sonny. And when I got home and told her, out came her photo album and there was Sonny with my mom again, and even a picture of him in new clothes, going home to Alert Bay. It never occurred to me as a kid, but I wonder now, if any of that made up to her for the economic desperation that forced her to work such long hard hours, looking after other people's kids while her own ran half wild.

Sometimes Klopinum and I would just walk along the edge of the water on the lip of dampness where the spindrift had dried and crackled under our feet with the stiff brown baked seaweed. Sometimes we followed the path into the bush, stepping from hot bright sunlight to cool shaded dampness, our feet squishing the underlay, sending up scents and smells and tastes it took me years to rediscover.

"Look," she'd say, "yellow vi'lets. Smell," she'd say, "thimbleberry leaves. Here," she'd say, "chew this," and when I did, it tasted like licorice, only sharper, fresher, not as sticky-sweet.

Sometimes we wouldn't talk at all, other times we both yapped and chattered. But the best times were when she told stories.

"Hear that?" she'd ask. "Old Raven sitting up in a snag, minding everyone else's business. Hear her? Bossing and scolding and giving advice nobody wants to hear. That Raven. . . ." And she'd smile, and there would be a story. "Raven is the trickster, she fools and gets fooled, her voice is a sharp stone that breaks the day. And one day, Raven. . . ."

"Sit on this log," she'd say, "and let's watch Snipe working for her dinner. You never see that Snipe wasting her time. But if you watch her long enough you'll see that even though she's working all the time, she's having fun too. Hear her talk talk talkin' to her family? Hear them talk, talk, talkin' right back, everybody out there busy, busy, busy and havin' such a good time. . . ."

"Oh Eagle," she'd shrug, "what's so great about Eagle? Just a big garbage truck is all Eagle is. Just another kind of sea gull except she can't swim like a Gull does. Now, if you want a bird, look at Osprey! She never eats somethin' that's been dead in the sun, never eats a thing she doesn't catch all herself. You don't see Osprey chewin' away on spawn dead salmon...."

"Here, you twist the heads off like this, then peel 'em like this, see? I'll show you one more time, and then you can do your own." The prawns, pink with red stripes, still steaming from the boiling sea water, dumped in the colander to drain, dripping onto the bare boards of the porch. We sat on the steps and shelled them all, ate a few dipped in butter, ate a few more. "All the small ones," she said, "are boys and all the big ones are female. See how they carry their eggs against them, between their legs, cuddled up so's the water won't wash 'em off too soon. The eggs are the best part, but you have to work for them, you have to suck and nibble and make all kinds of noise they wouldn't think polite at the church tea party." And she laughed gently, slurping deliberately loudly. "They all start off the same, they all start off boys, then when they're big enough, they change. Prawn has to be smart to get big. Smart ones get babies. Dumb ones are lunch for the fish. Dogfish are like that too. Start off as males, all the small, fast ones. When they're old enough and big enough, they change. The big females breed with a small male only maybe once every four, five years. Don't know how they manage that. Magic, I guess. The world is full of magic. It's everywhere. Dogfish breeds, but she doesn't have a bunch of eggs at once, not, say, like Frog or Salmon or most other things. Dogfish, her babies come out like blackberries. There's never a bush covered with nothing but ripe ones, you ever notice? Some green, some pink, some red, some maroon, some black. Dogfish, if you catch a female and open 'er up, she has one baby that's all set to be born, you can put it in the water and off it'll go, just a bit of egg sac left, and another almost as big but not quite, it might be able to swim, might not, and one a bit smaller, and smaller yet, right down to where there's just an egg with a little black dot in it. Every coupl'a days Dogfish has a baby. Magic. Lots of magic."

Klopinum wasn't much taller than I was, a round sturdy barrel of a Salish body and I have no idea at all how old she was that first summer. She wore brown lisle stockings and low-heeled shoes, a clean housedress with an apron over top, with pockets full of treasures. Her hair was almost snow white, no yellow streaks like some, and she kept it loosely pinned in a sort of a bun at the base of her neck. It escaped, often, and wisped softly around her head. "Oh, that hair," she'd say, "gettin' as hard to manage as a baby's." Her chubby short-fingered hands would reach back, the hair would tumble loose, briefly, then fingers flashing, she would do magic and the bun would be back, not a hairpin to be seen. Magic, the world is full of magic, it's everywhere. "There, that's better, drive me crazy otherwise. Here, straighten you up, too."

Klopinum had a round, flat face, her eyes almost lost in folds, wrinkles, creases, and her forehead was so prominent her eyes seemed hidden under the shelf of her brow. Her hands were gnarled, the skin wrinkled, and she ought to have been long past the age of running, ought to have been past the age to jump a beach log or clamber up a pile of rocks, but she did all that, and more. Laughing. "People forgot how to live, forgot a whole bunch of stuff, you want a good strong body, you have to teach it what you want it to do, otherwise you wind up livin' in an old wreck of a thing, not able to go anywhere any more. Don't tighten up when you run, you just run loose, and breathe like a dog. Your lungs go all the way down to your bellybutton, so don't breathe with your chest, breathe with your belly, fill up them lungs, use 'em properly. And if you get a bad cold, sniff warm sea water up your nose and wash all those germs out. It'll hurt, but not as bad as bein' sick hurts."

Everyone was so convinced death was waiting behind every rock, waiting to reach out and grab a kid and break everyone's heart.

My mother with her inoculations and dentists.

Klopinum with her sea water and dried roots.

My grandmother with her North English spring tonic and mustard plasters.

"Eat salmonberries, they're good for you, they're the first berries, they'll clean the winter out of your belly and you won't get sick."

She had made blackberry tarts, I remember that, so it was probably August, and so hot and still the dust hung in the air, the heat waves shimmered above the sea. Klopinum's fingers were stained blue with berry juice and her feet stuck out straight in front of her. We were sitting in the sand, leaning against a bleached log. Her shoes were canvas sneakers, gray, and almost finished.

Dzelarhons

Most of her stories I'd heard four or five or a dozen times and could almost recite word for word with her. "You tell a good story," she told me sometimes, and laughed softly. Sometimes, when the other Aunties came to visit, Klopinum would start a story, then nudge me sharply, and I knew I was expected to continue it for her. It was not expected that I use the very same words she used, but it was expected that whatever words I chose, the rhythm was to be as strong and as regular as the waves or my own breathing, and the heart of the story be unchanged. And when the story was done, nobody clapped, they nodded, and you knew inside yourself if you had done a good job of telling the story.

Most of the time the same basic story got told half a dozen different ways, variations on the same theme, but that August day Klopinum told me a story for the first time and then never told it to me again, although I asked for it often enough. "You'll remember it on your own," she answered. "You heard it when I told you, you know it, you don't need me to tell you that story."

She told me about the Creator. Not a man and not a woman but neither, and both, it doesn't matter. And there is no name other than the Creator, the Voice Which Must Be Obeyed. A good force, a good spirit, a good soul. The Creator. Made everything there is in this world and all other ones, made the birds and fish, the animals, trees, plants, rocks, flowers, and us, made it all, with love, and when everything was made and everything was alive, and the job all done, the Creator smiled. The Creator knew that nobody who lived would ever know everything or have all the answers, but everybody would always have questions. So the Creator took a little bit of the best of everything, and with it, the Creator made a rich river, and hid that river in everything. It's in me and it's in you and it's in that cedar tree and it's in that rock and it's in every grain of sand on this beach. A river of copper, because copper is sacred, comes in five colours, that's one more than magic. And all the holy people, all the sacred people, all the special people who have gifts are part of this river. The poets and the painters and carvers and singers, the dancers and drummers and storytellers, and everybody who walks and talks and breathes and lives in courage and in faith. And if you have love, and faith, and courage and trust and aren't afraid, you can find that river, and go to it, and drink Truth from it, and find some answers for yourself.

"You ought to write a book," I told her. "You could write a book and people would buy it and read the stories and it would be wonderful. Everybody would know your stories."

"No." Klopinum looked away and for a while didn't look or feel or sound like Klopinum at all, just an old woman with tired eyes. "Not me. Nobody wants those stories." She shrugged, then smiled, finally, and laughed. "I'm just an old klooch," and when I wanted to protest she shook her head. "Who listens to me? Who listens to us? Who listens? Anyway, I can't read and I can't write, and I never went to school and writers go to university."

"You could tell them and get someone else to write them," I insisted, as stubborn as anyone that age is. She just laughed, then reached out with her blackberry stained fingers, and took my hand in hers, and patted it. Patted. Patted. "You think so? Tell you what," she said, "I'll give them stories to you. You want it done, you do it."

When I was twelve I told my mother I was going to be a writer. When I was fifteen, and she was still working long hours for low pay, and there were four kids to feed instead of two, and money was more scarce than ever, my mother managed to save enough to buy me a typewriter. "You can't be a writer without one," she said.

Magic. The world is full of magic. It's everywhere. . . .

RAVEN AND SNIPE

Raven is a glutton.

No matter how much she has to eat, Raven is always hungry. But rather than work to feed herself, Raven prefers to resort to trickery. As often as not her tricks backfire on her.

Raven spends much of her time on the beach, looking for food and trying to find ways to trick the other birds and animals into feeding her. One day she noticed that Snipe always seemed to have a good supply of food. Snipe and her husband were busy from the time the sun came up until after it went back down again, gathering and storing food.

Raven wanted some of Snipe's food.

She went to where Snipe and her husband lived and looked at what they had gathered, stored, and preserved. Clams, oysters, berries, nuts, and fish of all kinds were dried, smoked, salted, and carefully stored for times of need.

Raven wanted some of that food.

In fact, Raven wanted all of that food!

Raven knew as well as anybody the rules of hospitality. And she decided to use these rules for her own benefit. Raven walked boldly up to Snipe's house and knocked on the door. When Snipe opened the door, Raven smiled. "Hello," she said, "I've come to visit you and Mr. Snipe and the children."

"Come in," said Snipe, opening her door wide and stepping aside to allow Raven to enter.

"Hello Mr. Snipe," said Raven politely, her sharp eyes noticing how well fed he was. "Hello all you little Snipes," she smiled, noticing how shiny their feathers were, how bright their eyes. "My," she said, "something in here smells good."

"Would you join us for supper?" Snipe asked, knowing full well Raven never said no to a free meal.

Raven smiled and nodded, and they all sat down to share food. "Thank you," the little Snipes said when their mother gave them their supper. "Thank you," said Mr. Snipe. "Thank you," said Raven. Then, while the others ate their meal quietly and politely, Raven started to feed herself. She gobbled and belched, she stuffed her beak and talked with her mouth full, she slobbered and drooled and reached with both hands, she picked up food with her fingers, she did everything except get her feet in the meal.

The Snipes could not believe what they were seeing.

Raven chomped and snoffled, she munched and burped, she smacked her lips and slurped and kept reaching for more, more, more.

Snipe realized Raven had no intention of leaving until every scrap of food was gone.

"We're very fortunate," Snipe said quietly, "we

24

always have an abundance of food."

"Yes," Raven belched, reaching for more.

"It's because my mother was a magic woman," Snipe confided. "A shaman who knew many mysteries."

"Really?" Raven slowed down, but she did not stop eating and gorping.

"Oh, yes," Snipe smiled. "Any time it looks as if we're running out of food, I just have to do some of the magic my mother taught me and we have more of everything."

"Really?" Raven was fascinated. "I don't suppose," she said with her mouth full, "there would be any way a person could talk you into sharing some of what your mother taught you."

"Oh, of course," Snipe smiled. "I'd be delighted. But I can't do the magic in the house, we have to go outside for that."

In a flash, Raven was away from the table, out of the house, and outside, waiting greedily to learn how to have an unlimited supply of food without ever having to do any work at all.

Snipe and her family went outside, carefully closing and locking the door so Raven could not get back inside to devour every scrap and morsel.

"First I'll light a fire," Snipe said. "Everybody gather up some dry wood so I can do my magic."

Raven raced around gathering wood, and, since she didn't know how big the fire had to be, she gathered all the wood she could find and piled it near Snipe's house. There was enough firewood there for months and months. The Snipe children smiled happily because it was their job to make sure there was always enough wood, and now Raven, without knowing it, had done much of the work for

25

them.

"When the fire is going," Snipe explained, "I have to dance through it four times. But nobody is to watch me do this. So while I am dancing, you have to keep your eyes shut, and concentrate."

Raven closed her eyes and concentrated. She thought of mountains of smoked salmon, piles of huckleberries and blackberries, mounds and heaps of nuts, and stacks and piles of oysters and clams.

"I'm dancing through the fire now," Snipe sang. But she only danced around it, and bent over to pick up some cool ashes to rub them on her feet and legs to make it look as if she had, in fact, danced in the fire.

She danced over to a log and pulled off a handful of soft moss. "I'm looking for a stone," she sang, "a sharp sharp stone, the sharper the better."

She danced over to where she had a secret stockpile of fish eggs, took a double handful of the fish eggs, and hid them inside the moss.

"You can open your eyes now, if you want," she said. Raven opened her eyes.

Snipe was dancing on the other side of the fire, and Raven couldn't see very clearly because of the bright light in her eyes. She squinted and peered, and through the smoke and the sparks saw Snipe with what looked like a very sharp, very pointed stone in her hand.

"I have to bang myself on the leg," Snipe explained. "I have to do it six times to complete the magic," and six times she raised the handful of moss filled with fish eggs, and brought it against her leg. Each time the moss touched her leg, she clacked her beak together, making a sound that convinced Raven Snipe really was bashing herself on the leg.

26

"Magic!" Snipe laughed, dropping the moss and lifting from it the double handful of fish eggs.

"Here," she handed the eggs to Raven who gobbled them down immediately.

"Would you teach me?" Raven asked, thinking that with this trick she would never again have to worry about food.

"Close your eyes," Snipe advised, and Raven closed her eyes. "Now dance," Snipe commanded.

Raven began to dance.

"Dance where I lead you," Snipe said, and Raven obeyed.

Snipe danced Raven to the edge of the fire, and then pointed Raven at the fire. "Dance forward," Snipe said, and Raven danced into the fire.

"Ow!" Raven screeched.

"Keep dancing!" Snipe called. "You have to remember this is Magic!"

Raven danced and hopped and squacked and yelled with pain and finally danced herself out of the fire.

"Turn around and come back," Snipe said, "you have to dance in the fire four times."

Raven wasn't feeling very enthusiastic about any of this, but she remembered all the food Snipe had, food Snipe said came from magic, and Raven, above all else, is a glutton.

She danced back into the fire, burning her legs and feet, singeing her feathers, cawing loudly in pain.

"Now the rock," Snipe said, choosing the biggest, heaviest, sharpest rock she could find. "Strike yourself on the leg as hard as you can; if it isn't done right, you won't get any food."

Raven took the rock, swung it as hard as she

could, and bashed herself on the ankle.

"Ouch!" she screamed.

"You'll have to do it again," Snipe said, almost laughing out loud. "You couldn't have done it hard enough because nothing happened."

"NO!" Raven yelled, weeping. "There has to be a better way to get food than this! I'm not doing this again, it isn't worth it!" and she ran away, crying bitterly.

The Snipes went back to work collecting, gathering, preserving, and storing food, making happy little noises as they worked, stopping often to remember how foolish Raven had been in her gluttony. And if, when you go to the beach, you move slowly and quietly, and find a comfortable place to sit, then sit very still and very quiet, Snipe and her family will begin to trust you, and you will be able to hear the happy noises they make as they work.

You may even hear Raven as she complains and protests enviously. But you will notice she never bothers the Snipes as they work.

RAVEN
GOES BERRYPICKING

R aven suggested to her friends Gull, Cormorant, and Puffin that they should all go berrypicking.

"We could use your dugout," she said to Cormorant, "and your paddles," she said to Gull, "and gather the berries in your baskets," she said to Puffin.

The friends agreed, and were nice enough not to ask Raven what it was she was going to provide.

Raven sat in Cormorant's dugout and smiled. "I'll hold the baskets," she offered, "so the rest of you can paddle," and the other three, knowing Raven, shrugged and handed her the baskets.

Raven enjoyed the ride, and amused the friends by describing to them all the scenery they were too busy to see and enjoy. "Oh," she said, "look below us, we are over an oyster bed. Why don't we dive for oysters?"

"Wonderful," the others agreed, glad of the chance

to stop pulling the paddles and working so hard.

"I don't swim," Raven smiled, "so I'll look after the dugout and you three can dive down and pry the oysters off the rocks and swim up to the surface with them, then I'll take the oysters and open them with my strong beak."

"Well," they thought, "at least she'll be doing Something for a change," and they agreed. One by one they dove over the side of the dugout and swam down to where the oysters clustered on the rocks. They pulled and pried and heaved and strained and managed to break off some, and, one by one, they swam back up to the surface and gave the oysters to Raven, who was lying in the dugout, floating on top of the water, humming a song to herself.

"Thank you," Raven smiled. "I'll open them while you go for more."

Finally, all three were tired and quite chilled by the water, and they swam up and climbed back into the dugout. Raven was lying resting on the baskets, burping and smiling, her belly round and tight as a drum.

"You've eaten them all!" Puffin accused.

"Not so," Raven denied. "See, there are six left; two for each of you." The three friends looked at each other and shrugged.

"Should have known," they told each other.

When they had rested and eaten their two oysters each, they picked up the paddles again, and started off looking for berries.

"Oh, look," said Raven from where she reclined against the baskets. "Look at all the sardines in the kelp beds. We could stop here and you could catch sardines and we could all share. I don't swim well, so I'll stay in the dugout and hang onto the kelp and keep the dugout from drifting away."

"Are you going to eat them all?" they asked, remembering the oysters.

"Of course not!" Raven said indignantly. "We will share equally. You can be sure of that."

So the trusting three went over the side again, and chased the sardines through the undersea forest of kelp.

When they had their beaks full, they swam up and dropped the sardines into the dugout.

"One for you," Raven said with a great big smile. "See, I'm putting this in your pile, Gull," and Gull, surprised but pleased, smiled and went back below the surface of the water to catch more. "And one for me," Raven laughed, popping a sardine in her mouth. "And one for Cormorant, and one for me, and one for Puffin, and one for me," and for every sardine she gave any of the others, she fed herself.

"We ought to have enough," Puffin said, "we've been fishing for over two hours."

They climbed back in the dugout and looked at the three little piles of sardines. "Is that ALL?" they said.

"Equal shares," Raven agreed, her belly swollen bigger than ever. "One for Gull and one for me and one for Puffin and one for me and one for Cormorant and one for me...."

"Trickster!" Puffin said, and Raven laughed. "You got three!"

"So did you," Raven reasoned.

"But there are three of us so it's only one each."

"Equal shares," Raven insisted, burping.

The three friends ate their sardines and glared at greedy Raven and vowed to themselves and each other that they weren't going to be tricked again.

They paddled to a small island and beached the

dugout on the shore, then took their baskets and began to gather berries. Salmonberries, huckleberries, blackberries, twinberries, salal berries, and oregon grapes, they gathered and stored in their baskets.

Raven picked berries too, but she didn't put hers in the basket. She ate the ones she picked. She munched and she crunched and she chewed and she swallowed and she gorped and she stuffed herself until even she thought she was going to split right down the middle.

"Ooooooooooh," she moaned.

"What's wrong?" asked Puffin.

"Oh, I feel TERRIBLE!" Raven moaned.

"Small wonder," Cormorant said with absolutely no sign of sympathy at all.

"Gluttony is its own worst enemy," Gull pontificated.

"Got what you deserved," little Puffin muttered.

"Oh, I can't pick any more berries," Raven groaned. She hobbled to the dugout and lay down in it, but she couldn't get comfortable. She grizzled and whined and moaned and complained and felt very sorry for herself the whole time the others were picking berries.

"My baskets are full," said Puffin.

"Mine too," said Gull.

"Mine too," said Cormorant.

"Raven's aren't full, we can use them, she isn't going to be picking any more berries today, she's too sick," Puffin suggested.

So the other three picked until even Raven's baskets were full.

And the whole time they were working, Raven was moaning with bellyache.

They loaded the baskets into the dugout and got in. "I can't paddle," Raven gasped, "I'm too sick."

"Figures," Puffin grumbled.

Raven lay in the dugout feeling sorry for herself while the others did all the work. "I'm so thirsty," she whined, "I have got to have a drink of water or I'll die."

So the other three paddled to a place where there was fresh water.

"I can't walk to the pool," Raven protested.

"She's up to something," Puffin warned.

"She's not feeling well," Cormorant defended.

"She's up to something," Puffin insisted.

But the three friends went to get Raven a drink of water. While they were gone, Raven ate all the berries in the baskets she hadn't filled herself.

"I told you," Puffin said when she saw the empty baskets.

"You loaned those baskets to me," Raven argued, "so the berries in them were mine."

"You didn't pick them!" Gull said very very angrily. "We picked them!"

"They were my baskets," Raven insisted stubbornly.

Raven drank the water they had brought and then lay down and put her wing over her eyes. "The sun," she said, "it's hurting my eyes. Oh, I feel so terribly ill."

"Here," said Cormorant, "we'll pile these baskets and you can lie in the shade."

"She's up to something," Puffin warned again.

"What can she do now, sick as she is?" Cormorant asked.

"She's up to something."

And while the other three did all the paddling,

35

Raven poked a hole in a basket and ate the berries. When that basket was empty, she started on another basket.

"Look at that," Puffin whispered to Gull and Cormorant. "See what she's up to now?"

"Glutton," said Cormorant.

"Trickster," said Gull.

"She isn't the only one who can play tricks," Puffin said. And she dug her paddle deep into a wave and turned the dugout sideways so the sun hit Raven right in the eyes.

"Oh, oh, oh," Raven wailed. "Oh, the sun gives me a headache."

"Here," Puffin said, "throw this blanket over your head and shade your eyes." And Raven did.

Immediately Puffin jumped up, pulled a strong cord from where it had been stored, and tied Raven inside the blanket. And to be sure no more of the berries disappeared, she took two turns around Raven's greedy beak. "There," she said with satisfaction, "that'll hold you." And to be sure that it did, she jumped up and down on Raven.

Inside the blanket, Raven began to sweat until she sweated out all the water she had been given. She even sweated out the juice of all the berries she had eaten. She became very very thirsty and very sad. She sweat and sweat until she really did have a bellyache and a headache and her eyes really did hurt. All the things she had pretended to have wrong with her actually did go wrong, and she was very very ill.

When they got back to the village they stood up and dropped their paddles on the blanket-wrapped Raven and gave her lumps, bumps, and bruises. "Oh, oh, oh," Raven cried. "Why are you doing this to me?"

"Because you are a glutton," said Gull.

"Because you are a cheat," said Cormorant.

"Because you are always up to something," said Puffin.

They told all the other creatures all the things Raven had done. "Either we will banish you and nobody will ever talk to you again or play with you or be friends with you, or you will have to make up for what you've done," the creatures decided.

Raven didn't want to live her life all alone. "Anything," she said. "I'm sorry, I truly am."

"Not as sorry as you are going to be," little Puffin promised.

For four days they took Raven back to the berry island, and Raven had to do all the work. She had to paddle the dugout and go over the side for oysters, she had to catch sardines and then fill all the berry baskets while the others lay in the sun and enjoyed life. And to be sure Raven didn't eat anything, they tied her beak up with the strong cord Puffin had provided.

"I'm sorry," Raven repeated, but nobody listened to her.

"I'll be good," she promised, but nobody listened.

"I've learned my lesson," she vowed, but the three friends looked at each other and then at Raven.

"She's up to something," said Puffin.

"She's already figuring out another trick," said Gull.

"She's got that look in her eye," said Cormorant.

Raven flew to the top of a tree and sat in it feeling very lonely and sad. "Nobody trusts me," she cawed to herself. "Nobody trusts me at all."

ORCA'S CHILD

Long ago, Orca was only one colour, black, and she lived like all the other sea mammals, living in the water, coming to the surface to breathe.

Sometimes, she would lie on top of the chuck and watch Eagle Flies High riding the wind.

Eagle Flies High isn't any bigger than any other eagle, but she is strong, and she flies higher and further, for longer periods of time, and she giggles and laughs at the things she sees below her.

Orca began to wonder what it would be like to fly in the air instead of swimming in the chuck. She watched Eagle Flies High swoop to the surface of the sea and rise back up again with Salmon caught in her strong feet, and Orca began to feel that Eagle Flies High was her special friend.

When Orca saw Eagle Flies High approaching, Orca would dive down to where Salmon lives, and she would chase Salmon up to the surface so Eagle Flies High could catch her food easily.

When Eagle Flies High realized what Orca was doing, she'd swoop over the waves, calling a thank you, telling of the things Orca would never experience, of snow high on the mountains, of small flowers in the meadows, of bushes thick with berries and of sunlight slanting through the columns of the forest.

Orca told Eagle Flies High that she had never seen a flower, and Eagle Flies High brought a foxglove and dropped it to her. Another time she brought Lupin, another time Dogwood, and when the berries were ripe, Eagle Flies High brought some for Orca to try.

Orca and Eagle Flies High became very good friends, and their friendship grew until they loved each other so strongly it was as if light came from their bodies when they saw each other.

But one was a creature of the air, and one was a creature of the sea, and neither could live in the world of the other.

Still, they loved each other, and love has a way of making sure it gets shown and expressed. Orca wanted so badly to know what it felt like to fly, fly as her love did, that she began to jump high out of the water, until there was no other creature in the sea who could leap as high.

And Eagle Flies High spent more and more of her time closer and closer to the surface of the waves, that she might be close to her love.

And one day, as Eagle Flies High swooped towards the waves, Orca leaped into the air and for one moment, their bodies touched, and their love was shown.

When their child was born, she was black like
Orca, but with white on her body, like the head and
tail of Eagle Flies High, and she could make piping
sounds like the bird did, and she giggled.

Orca loved her baby and taught it everything a
whale child should know, and Eagle Flies High tried
to teach her to fly. But the new baby, though she
could leap higher and further than her mother, and
spent much more time out of the sea than any other
creature, could not learn to fly.

Still, the black and white baby loved to leap and
jump, to giggle and sing, and to play games of every
sort. No other whale enjoys life quite as much as
Orca, and every new Orca baby that's born has white
patches, and they're different on every new whale,
no two the same.

And because these wonderful creatures are the
result of love between creatures of different worlds,
they are capable of love for all things.

There is a place on the west coast of Vancouver
Island where the rocks stick way out into the sea,
and in the old days, the women would go out there at
certain times of the year, in the spring and in the
fall, when Orca is moving up and down the coast.

The women would sit on the rocks and play their
flutes and whistles.

Orca does not hear only with her ears, as we do.
Every inch of skin on Orca's body picks up sound
vibrations, and she not only hears the music, she
feels it as well.

And when Orca heard and felt the music of the
women, she would swim to the place where the
rocks stick far out into the chuck, and she would rise
up, up, up, out of the waves, until she was balanced

only by her mighty tail flukes, and, with most of her body exposed to the sight of the women, she would sway to the music.

Then the women would hear the most beautiful of sounds, a sound so wonderful there are no words to describe it, a sound so full of love and truth it brought tears to the eyes, tears of happiness. The sound of Orca singing.

And the women would listen to Orca, as Orca had listened to the flutes and whistles, and sometimes, for a magical moment, the women would play their flutes as Orca sang, and the music of two different realities would blend and merge, and all creation would listen. It is said that at these times Osprey would fly up, up, up, her patterned underside exposed to view, and she would add her song to the chorus, and three realities would be joined in speech. And when this happened, the very rocks of the earth would begin to vibrate, and hum, until all of creation, for a brief moment, was united.

Then, with a final sound, Orca would splash back into the water to continue her voyage. And anyone splashed by a whale has luck, and will have happiness, for this is one of the blessings of Orca, whose very body bears the marks of a love that found its expression and blended two very different realities.

MUDDLEHEAD

Now it is known that the world is so old our minds cannot even begin to understand. It is said if you took one stick for every year the world has been, and if you piled those sticks together, you would have a heap taller than any mountain. It is said if you lit this pile of sticks with fire, the flames would reach to the sky and the light of that fire would banish night from the entire world for so long there would be people born, live, and die of old age without ever having seen darkness. And that is how old they say this world is.

In a span of time like that, it is not surprising that stories are lost, people are dispersed and those who once were of the same family wind up thinking themselves strangers. Events happen in one place and not another place, and so the way one group of people keep time might well differ from the way another group of people keep time. What is known by some is this; as a frog grows, it sometimes needs to shed its skin, splitting along the back, the old skin peeling off, the frog stepping from her old discard in a new skin. And the world was made from the discards of Frog Woman, and floated on her back while she slept. Some say the world grew on the shell of Turtle Woman, and it may be that is the truth. Others say the world was formed from mud and dust gathered by Spider Woman and rolled into a ball. However it happened, and whichever story is true, obviously somehow, the world was made.

And it was made all in one piece. Then something happened, and bits of the edge of the world broke loose, to become islands, and this separated the People. Until that time, we were all one family, and nobody was greater or lesser, nobody was richer or poorer, nobody was better than anybody else.

But when the very world as you know it changes, when knowledge is lost and you cannot depend on anything, things change, and not always for the better.

There was the great earthquake, which separated the people, and there were volcanic eruptions, which dispersed the survivors, and there was a flood which covered the face of the entire earth, and each of these terrible events killed many people, whose stories died when they did. But it is known by some that the rock carvings were done either just before or just after one of the disasters, probably the earthquake, and were done before any of the dispersed people found their way back here.

And it is known that often, when the dispersed arrived back, they were amazed to find people living here, and in those times, the people living here did not look the way they look today. But they married or were mixed in with the newcomers, and their children began to look like the newcomers, and the differences were lost. It is known that the people who were first here and who were not dispersed were a lighter-skinned people, and that they did the rock carvings, and that is almost all that is remembered of them. But sometimes, a person is seen who is just a little bit paler, or has hair of a slightly different colour, or eyes that are not as dark. And that is the proof that somewhere, years and years ago, longer ago than we can remember, one of their foremothers or forefathers was of the first people here.

And when you think how old this world is, and how many people have lived through all those years and all those happenings, nothing is very surprising.

When the world was apportioned it was understood that everything is part of everything and there is nothing that can stand alone or live without food; everything feeds off everything else. And it was known that the taking of life is a very serious thing, and that if you kill something, you are required by obligation to eat it, or to use it. You commit atrocity if you kill and waste, or if you make dirty the water, or treat things with no respect. It was also understood that not everything thinks the same way; what is important to one form of life might not be important to another, so it is not always easy to live in any kind of harmony. Obeying the laws of respect makes it easier to live in harmony.

And so it was some rules were devised, and one rule has to do with bears and people. The bears promised that they would not creep silently through the bush, as do the cougars, but would, instead, lumber and crash so we could hear them coming and get out of their way. And we, in turn, promised we would not move silently either, or startle the bear, or place ourselves between a mother and her cubs, or frighten them into thinking they had to defend themselves. And we also promised we would not be careless with food, and leave it lying around to tempt the bear, then become angry if the bear came and got it. We promised, also, that no woman having her time of menstruation would go into the hills to pick berries or such, for the smell of a bleeding woman reminds the bears of the smell of a she-bear in season, and when they smell that beautiful odour, they can no longer think. We also promised that we would sing when we were near a bear trail, and wear a bell if we had one, to warn the bears we were there, and that way they would know we were not out hunting them.

And one bear story is about the woman who became mother to bear cub children. Some people, when they tell the story, have a name for this young woman, others don't, and some of the names are not the same so perhaps this story happened in more than one place to more than one person.

This young woman was what might be called a Muddlehead. She talked a lot, but said little, and whatever was the latest idea, she was the first to expound it. She never settled herself at any task long enough to become an expert, but was quick to find fault with anything anyone else did. She would go out with the ones gathering firewood, but never gather as much as the others. Instead she would talk, and laugh, and chatter, and tell others how the job ought to be done, and if anyone suggested she was not working very hard, she would become angry, and would often weep and accuse the others of being cruel to her. If there was anything going on at all, she had to appear to be a part of it, and if anyone came from another village to visit, this young woman had to make it appear she was important to the visitor in some way.

We have all met people like that. Muddleheads.

Well, this young woman went out with two others to pick huckleberries, and because the best berries grow higher up the hills than the villages are usually built, they climbed up with their berry baskets, which they wore on their backs, and which were kept in place by a backstrap which went around their foreheads, leaving their hands free to gather the fine berries.

And up they climbed, with two of the young women singing a song to tell the bears they were coming. And the third woman, the Muddlehead, talking and laughing, and assuring the other two how much they would enjoy the berry picking, and telling stories about other people, stories which all, somehow, reflected credit on her rather than on the others.

Now, when you are picking berries, as anyone knows, there are areas which are not for us, and those areas are marked by the bears, who drop their dung as a sign that they have laid claim to certain bushes. But this Muddlehead paid no attention to that, and picked wherever it was she decided was where she wanted to pick. Talking all the time, and laughing, laughing, laughing, chattering away like a crow, laughing at nothing at all, and soon the other two paid her no attention at all, because what she was saying was just silliness.

But the bears heard her. They were lying in a cool

shady place, their bellies full of berries, and they could hear this chatter, and all this giggling and empty laughing. They peered out at the berry pickers and saw the two women talking quietly to each other, talking clearly and slowly, and not babbling and giggling. And they saw the third one, off by herself, picking berries from bushes clearly marked as being the bears' bushes. "Well," they said, "look at that, she steals our berries, and she laughs. She is not talking to the other two, and it is inconceivable a woman would talk to a huckleberry bush, so she must be talking to us. And she is laughing, laughing, laughing, picking our berries, saying words we cannot understand, and laughing. She mocks us," they decided.

Well, they could have come thundering out of the bushes right then and there and done something dreadful, but it was a nice day, and they had full bellies, and the other two weren't doing anything outrageous, so they waited, but they were insulted, and very angry.

In the afternoon, the two sensible women picked berries and stopped only for a small meal and a drink of water, but the Muddlehead, true to her wasteful nature, took a long rest. She nibbled on smoked fish and ate only the best parts, tossing what she didn't want over her shoulder, into the bushes, right under the noses of the bears. She ate some cured oysters, and ate only the soft middle part and threw the dry outer part after the smoked fish. And the bears could smell all this food, but all they could find were only the little bits and scraps, and that only made them hungrier and angrier.

When evening came, the three started down the hillside path, two of them with full baskets balanced properly, and the Muddlehead with her half-full basket slung over one shoulder. Knowing what you know of her personality, you can just about imagine what the downward trip was like. She was tired, she had a sore back, she had a headache from too much sun, and her basket was too heavy. She was hungry, her feet were sore, and would someone please help her carry the heavy basket. On and on. Finally, one of the other two women said, quite sharply, because she was absolutely tired of all the nattering and whining, "Just stop complaining and do what needs doing." Well, of course, the Muddlehead got angry. Accused the other of not being very kind. The other said, "If you're tired, it's probably because you haven't stopped bouncing around chattering and being silly all day. If your back seems sore, it's probably from lying on it all afternoon. If you have a headache from too much sun, you might remember next time to bring your hat. And if your basket seems heavy, maybe it's because you aren't carrying it properly!"

The Muddlehead started whining and crying and talking about how nobody ever understood her, and how everyone always treated her shabbily, and she was so busy feeling sorry for herself and enjoying the tears slipping from her eyes, she didn't see the pile of bear dung on the path. She stepped in it. With her bare feet.

Well, every annoyance or anger she'd ever felt burst out because of the bear dung. She ranted and raved about it, and wound up saying every bear that had ever walked that path was so stupid it didn't know who its mother and father were. Which is the worst insult you can give to a bear. Or a person, probably. "Too stupid," she said, "to even step off the path and leave their mess in the salal, too stupid to have any idea how to behave." And she grabbed her basket, swung it roughly to her back, and broke the backstrap. The other two just kept walking. "Help me fix this," the Muddlehead demanded. "You broke it," one said, "you fix it, we've got a long way to go with heavy baskets full of berries, and we want to get back before dark."

Well, the Muddlehead wasted a lot of time crying and whining and then she made a half-hearted effort to fix the packstrap, but it didn't hold together because she'd never really bothered to learn how to do anything properly, and in the end she was forced to carry the basket in her arms, held against her body. Which meant she couldn't move very easily and was always just a little bit off balance. Instead of singing softly to warn the bears, she grumbled and muttered, and each time she skipped or stumbled, she complained that it was probably because of the bear dung on the path, and all the fault of the stupid bears, who ought not to be allowed to get in people's way.

She stopped to rest, and was feeling very sorry for herself when two very large, obviously strong young men came from the bushes and saw her. The two young men looked so much alike, she was certain they were brothers, maybe even twins. "Please," she said, snivelling a bit and trying to smile so she would look pretty, and dependent, and helpless, and needy. "Please, this basket is broken, and I am very tired, and it's getting dark and this path is ankle deep in bear droppings and I keep slipping and stumbling. Please," she said, "will you help me."

One brother looked at the other and they both smiled. And one brother picked up the basket as easily as if it were nothing at all, and the other took her by the arm, and they started off together.

"Oh," said the young woman, "but we are going uphill instead of downhill," but neither of the brothers said anything. "Where are you taking me?" she whined, and they just kept on walking. She noticed, then, that these two powerful twin brothers were not dressed as were the men in her village, but wore only very shaggy, roughly made robes of bearskin. And then she noticed that they were very hairy men, with bearded faces, and thick body hair and even hair on their arms and legs. "Oh," she said, "and if you are bandits, my people will come after you." But the brothers didn't say a word, and though she tried to pull loose, it did not do one bit of good, they were so powerful that they just kept pulling her with them. She pleaded, she wept, she cajoled, and she hollered, and none of it made any difference. Soon they came to an enormous house built into the side of the mountain, and the two men took her inside.

A small fire burned in the middle of the house, and around it a family of people were sitting, having supper. And every one of them looked like every other one of them, men and women alike, stocky, powerful, and very very hairy, and each and all of them wearing the same kind of bearskin tunic.

Then the two young men began to speak to the others, but not in words, or at least not in words the Muddlehead could understand. Growls and grunts and great snappings of teeth, and when one of them skidded his foot on the floor deliberately and pretended to stumble and slip, and flailed his arms and started to whine and mewl, and all the others laughed, the young woman understood everything.

55

These two were not men at all, but bears, and they were telling the others how she had behaved, what had happened, and how stupid she appeared when she slipped in the bear dung.

Then the one telling the story about her turned, and walked to stand right in front of her and when he spoke, she understood what he meant, even if she didn't understand the individual words. "Marry me or die," is what he said.

Weeping did no good at all, howling and wailing only made them laugh, and running away was the worst idea of all. They just reached out, sank their huge curved claws into her back, and dragged her easily. Easy for them, hard on her.

Finally, she agreed, and she apologized, and she did everything she could to try to make them think well of her, until, finally, they all nodded and let her sit by the fire, and gave her some raw fish to eat.

But then all the others went to bed and left her alone with this young bear man who was now her husband. As we all know, or if we do not know we can certainly imagine, animals are not built the same way as people and it was never intended by creation that they mate together. The bear sat with his legs apart, and he grabbed the young woman, and he sat her down, almost, but not quite, on his lap. She wept, again, and she did not like the smell of him, nor the feel of his hairy body, and she certainly did not like the way he handled her. And when the bear finally lay down and went to sleep, the Muddlehead was exhausted, and aching from his rough embraces.

It didn't take very long, and the young Muddlehead knew she was pregnant. She was afraid to have her family know, and afraid to stay with the bear. Every day, she heard her family out searching for her, calling her name, making a noise to attract her attention, and with half her heart she wanted to run to them. With the other half she wanted to run away from them, so that they not know what the bear had done with her and to her.

So she dithered. It is better to do almost anything at all than dither. While she was dithering, the bear made his own decision. He told his family he was taking her even higher up the mountain, up past the place where there is only bare rock, up past the place where even dogs would not be able to smell her scent, and so he just lifted her up, tucked her under his arm, and headed off into the hills. Every time he passed a stand of devil's club, he ripped pieces of it to shreds and scattered it all over his back trail, so that if any dogs were following him, their noses and heads would get so badly hurt they would run away and leave him alone.

When they finally got to a big cave near the top of the mountain the bear put his wife on some soft branches and gathered firs and dry grass and did everything he could to make her comfortable. When she was finally sleeping, he did as much magic as he could do, so that when she wakened he wasn't as ugly and bear-like as he had been. He was still far from being handsome, but at least he wasn't so furry and rough. And his mouth was shaped enough like a person's that he could at least speak to her. He stayed in man form until it was time for him to go hunting and then he did magic, and became a bear again, and changed back to man after he had captured food and returned to the big cave.

Some days she would hear her brother's dogs barking, looking for her, but she was so huge with pregnancy, and so swollen and changed, she could not even get the energy to call for help. The bear hunted for her, and did everything he could to make her comfortable, but she was sick, and she was miserable, and no wonder, either, because never has a woman been as swollen with pregnancy as that Muddlehead woman. By the time her twin cubs were born she was so sick she hardly even felt the birth pains.

The two children, though half bear, were her children and she loved them. She knew it was not through any sin or fault of their own that they were what they were. She nursed them, she sang to them, she cared for them, and every day she loved them more. The bear, watching her, began to feel some measure of love for her. Not much, but some. And he thought that perhaps she was no longer the kind of person she had been when he captured her. Which didn't mean he was the least bit sorry for what he had done.

One day, when the bear was hunting, the Muddlehead's brother arrived with his dogs, searching for the Muddlehead woman, and the dog smelled her scent on the fur of the large bear catching fish in the stream. The dog raced toward the bear, and the bear, alarmed, stood on his hind legs, ready to fight. But the brother called the dog back and said, "No, dog, we aren't here to bother the fishing bears, we are here to find my sister," and the dog tried to explain, but the brother did not understand.

The bear left, and went back to the cave and told the Muddlehead what had happened. "Sooner or later," he said, "your brother will become at least as smart as his dog, and then I will probably die." The Muddlehead woman could hardly say she was barely able to wait for that day to arrive, because she was still quite afraid of the bear and knew he had a vicious temper, but she began to hope her brother would get as smart as his dog. She began to make things for the bear, things which she held in her hands and covered with her scent, and she took to brushing his fur and grooming him, not because she loved him, but because she wanted her brother's dogs to smell her scent on him. And every day she prayed her brother would become as clever as his hunting dogs.

When the snow was on the ground the brother and his dogs approached the place where the bear had his cave. And the Muddlehead knew she had to do something, there was no time left for dithering. She made a snowball and pressed it hard with her hand, leaving fingermarks on it, human fingermarks, and she threw it down the hillside where the dogs saw it and began to bark and yap.

They looked up, up, looking for the place the snowball had been thrown from, and they saw the dark mouth of the cave against the white of the snow, and the brother, who had become at least as smart as his dogs, said, "There, there is where she is!"

And the bear came from the cave and said, "Wait. You are my brother-in-law whether you know it or not. I know you are going to kill me, and we both know there is no changing that. But allow me, at least, to sing my death song, so that my children can learn it and teach it to their children, and know who I was and that I loved them."

And the brother said, "Fine, then, sing your song." The bear did, and he danced, and then he lifted his sons and cuddled them and said, "You will be the strongest of all men, and you will be brave and powerful, and know, always, that you are the children of the bears."

Then he put them down and the brother-in-law killed him. The two boys wept to see their father dead, but when their mother and her brother started down the mountainside, the bear children went with them, and all the way down they sang a song that told of the death of the father. All other bears, hearing this, wept, and knew what had happened, and knew not to go out on the path until the people had gone.

THE BEARDED WOMAN

A̲t one time, before the disasters happened that fractured the earth and turned reality upside down, things were done in certain ways, and then, sometimes, through natural disaster, sometimes because the people had lost sight of the way things were supposed to be done, the ways of doing things changed, and what had never been considered, became accepted.

Many of the people, particularly the ones who remained here, lived as fishers, hunters and gatherers, and did not till the land, but rather harvested the natural bounty. Other people, perhaps because they could not depend on such richness from their coasts and waters, began to plant gardens, began to herd and tend animals, began to think of land as something to use, something to keep for themselves.

The women, possibly because they were the ones who would grow large, slow, and clumsy with pregnancy and were the ones who would not be able to move as far or as freely with infants and small children to care for, established villages where their families could be raised in safety, and in those villages the women tended the crops, herded the fowl and domesticated animals, and learned the skills of weaving, pottery, and medicine. A woman who was an expert in those things would teach her daughters everything she knew, and her sons would go to stay with their uncles, to learn the hunting skills of the men. The house in which the family dwelt, and all that there was inside it, belonged to the woman, and through her, to her children, and the men were either in the house of their mother, or living in the house of a woman who wanted a husband. Sometimes, for different reasons, several women would share a house, dividing the work among them, sometimes sharing even the same husband to be father to their children. Or, if a woman preferred to live with only her children, and not to have a man around all the time, that was also how it was done, and accepted.

Then something happened, and it is not known what it was that caused the changes. Over a period of years and generations, many things got turned upside-down and inside-out, and then it was that a woman did not inherit anything from her mother, everything was passed from father to son, and only to the oldest son, the others being expected to make their own way in the world. This led to many fights and arguments between brothers, and even to murder and war. And a daughter could inherit from her father only if there were no living male heirs. If a woman did inherit, and did have title to a house and land, her chances of keeping her patrimony were very slight, for all any man had to do to gain control was to rape her in front of witnesses. Then, according to law, she was his wife, whether she agreed or not, and everything that had once been hers was his.

And so it was a woman lost her land, and was forced to be wife to a man who had never asked her permission, and the woman watched this man ruling over everything that had once been hers.

When her first child was born, it was a girl, and the woman was happy, but the father, of course, wanted a son. And so he tried again to get his wife pregnant, and he succeeded, and she again had a daughter. For all the years they lived together, the only children the woman gave birth to were daughters, and the man became desperate for sons. He went with servant women, and if they did not want to, forced them, and with some of the servant women he had sons, but the law and the religion said these sons were bastards and could not inherit. So the father said, "Well, and what I will do, then, is marry these sons to my daughters, then even if I die and the land and wealth goes to a girl, she will be married and it will all work out in the end. My son will control everything."

The oldest daughter knew she would be the first one to be forced into a marriage and she was not interested in living such a life. She knew she had no choices or options, there was no work a woman could do in those days except the meanest and most shameful sort, and a woman might till the fields all day and not be given even a good meal. Then, after all that work and little food, she could still be taken by any man who decided he wanted to use her. And so the oldest daughter killed herself.

The second daughter knew that all that meant was it would be she who was forced into an unnatural marriage, and she was no more eager than her dead sister, so the second daughter ran away, and the father was furious, and publicly disinherited her and said she was dead and no child of his.

The third daughter did not want to kill herself, and had no intention of running away and abandoning her old mother. Nor did she have any intention of being disinherited and so she studied the matter carefully and she learned what it was a man wanted in a wife, and what it was he did not want in a wife.

The first thing she learned to do was talk from the bottom of her throat instead of from the top. Her voice became very soft, very low, and not at all the high, thin voice the men said they liked. Then she changed her bodily appearance, and every day, for hours, she exercised, until she had long strong muscles in her arms and legs, and her hands were dark-tanned and obviously used to work. She did not look nor move like the delicate kind of women the men said they liked.

But even moving like a sleek cat and talking in a low soft voice was not enough. Her brothers mocked her and said she was ugly and stupid and no kind of real woman at all, but they also said the oldest one would marry her all the same because of the land and the wealth.

And so the third daughter went into seclusion for many days and weeks. She ate only enough to keep herself alive, she drank only enough to keep her body healthy, and she considered, prayed, thought and meditated. And when she came out from the room, all who saw her stared in wonder and shock. On her face, she was growing fine hair, and she made no effort at all to get rid of it. The servants stared, and couldn't think of a thing to say. Her mother gasped and it wasn't until the young woman explained the reason for this that her own mother could begin to accept the unusualness of it. The father roared with rage that a daughter of his should grow a beard, but what could anyone do about it; even the wisest had no idea how to stop hair from growing.

Not one of the brothers wanted to marry a woman with a beard. "Well, then," said their father, "I will marry her off to someone else, and leave all my wealth to my grandchildren." And he, himself, because he trusted nobody with so important a task, set out to find a husband for the young woman with the beard.

While her father was gone, the young woman, who was not the least little bit interested in getting married and seeing all the wealth and land go to someone she did not even know, occupied herself with the business of running the place that had once belonged to her mother. Every day she was up early, and out, and working, and not only did she work steadily and hard, she made the others work too. Now, for most of the people, work was nothing new, they had been doing it all their lives, with no thanks, and no pay, and only a bare subsistance of food. But for the brothers, work was something they did not want to have to learn about, and so two of them went off to join the army, where they could have a good time killing and plundering, and the third, who had no taste for the army, went into the church and spent his life praying to a god nobody knew very well, and even fewer people understood.

That left more food for the others, and with all the

work they were all doing, the crops grew and were harvested, the animals grew fat, and life became somewhat more pleasant. They all ate together, and they all ate the same and the days when the father and his sons would eat the meat and the others get soup made from the bones were finished.

The father travelled everywhere looking for a husband for his daughter, and finally, he found one who pleased him, and spoke to him of the matter, and an agreement was made, and they rode back together. The father had not bothered to mention the small matter of his daughter's beard, and in the time he had been gone, the beard had continued to grow. The prospective husband looked at the daughter, and could not believe what he was seeing. He had expected to see the daughter of a rich man, a woman with a thin, high voice, a woman dressed in fine clothes, a woman who was dainty, and instead, he was looking at a tall young woman with a beard, a tall young woman with strong hands and tanned face, a woman dressed in rough pants and a work shirt, her body made hard and strong by hours of work. And always, of course, the matter of the beard.

The agreement was forgotten, the prospective husband returned to his own family, and everywhere he went, he told the story of the man who had tried to trick him into marrying a woman with the muscles of a worker and a beard on her chin.

The father raged and roared and screamed and yelled, and thought he would beat his daughter into behaving properly. He got a stick and went after her with it, but she took it from him and said, "Father, you are not going to beat me with that stick." "Well," he said, "never mind the stick, then," and he pulled back his fist to hit her. She took him by the wrist, and twisted, and forced him to his knees, and she said no. That is all she said. No.

Everyone who saw what happened told someone else, and those people told other people, and soon it was known far and wide that the young woman with the strong body and the bearded chin had bested her father and told him no.

The second sister, who had run away rather than get married, heard the tale and returned home. She was ragged and hungry, she was tired and sad, she had been abused and misused and made to work long hours for nothing more than a few scraps of food and some mouldy hay to sleep on, and yet, when she arrived home, her mother knew her and so did her sister.

They wept for and with her, fed her substantial meals, gave her clean, warm clothes and cared for her bastard child as if it were a legitimate heir. Even the little boy's grandfather seemed relieved and even proud of him, and often managed to bring himself to speak kindly to the child.

The returned sister often stared at the little beard and then looked away quickly, eyes welling with tears, and finally, one day, said to her younger sister that perhaps they could find a healer or a sorcerer, or someone who might know how to get rid of the disfigurement. The childless sister stared, as if she could not understand what was being said to her, and then shook her head. "Why," she asked, "would I want to get rid of the very thing that has been my salvation?" The older sister, who had run away and returned when it appeared to be safe, gently pointed out that the beard was unattractive. The younger sister grew very angry, but she loved her sister too much to kick her over the moon, so she took several deep breaths instead, and then said, in a carefully controlled voice, that she did not find her beard at all unattractive. "It has kept me," she said, "from having to venture out into a world full of people who wanted only to abuse me. It has kept me from hunger, from exploitation, from rape, from fear and from homelessness. You," she continued, "have strands of white in your hair even though you are still a young woman. Your face is lined, your eyes are dark with sorrow, and you have been too long away from home. I would far sooner have my beautiful little beard than your sad history, and I think my lovely little tuft far more beautiful than the nightmares which still waken you or the hollow sound which has replaced your laughter."

The older daughter, of course, felt sorry for her younger sister, and never did manage to make herself understand why it was the unmarried woman carefully tended her beard, washing it, even carefully curling it and rubbing it with rosewater and sometimes even lemon balm.

The father died, and the illegitimate brothers returned to try to claim the land. The bearded young woman met them and explained to them that the land had belonged first to her mother, and never to their father or their respective mothers, and she said the brothers had no claim on the land. They fell to fighting among themselves, first with fists, then with knives, and when they were all either badly wounded or weakened by strife, she went to them again, and said the same thing, that they were fighting for something which was not theirs. Even weakened as they were, they thought they could at least defeat her, a mere woman, even if she did have a beard, and, enraged by her words, they attacked her, only to find she was, indeed, as strong as any worker, and besides, she was assisted by many of the people who lived on the family land and worked it, and were even paid for their work. The brothers left, and two of them re-joined the army and were killed in a battle over something that nobody can remember. The one who had been a religious returned to his order and spent his days muttering prayers and imploring the god nobody knew very well to in some way assure that justice was done.

And it might be that this god who was a stranger to most of the people heard these prayers and granted them, for the three women lived out their days on the land, and, in time, the bastard son of the older sister was recognized as the heir. And when the younger sister was finally buried, it is said her little beard was snow white and curled gently from her beautiful aged face, reaching almost to her waist, and her nephew refused to allow anyone to shave it off, saying his aunt had lived long on the earth with her treasure, and it was only fitting she still have it when she arrived in heaven.

Ta-Naz Finds Happiness

J ohn Richardson thought he had never been so miserable in his life. The wind howled like a wild animal, a wild animal caged and demanding freedom. The waves were mountainous and capped with angry white froth, the rain pelted like sharp needles, and the deck was slippery under his bare feet. Every time he thought he had regained his balance, another wave would crash against the side of the ship and send him staggering all over again. Clouds hid the moon and somewhere in that terrible blackness was the rocky shoreline of what sailors called "The Graveyard of the Pacific." More ships had smashed against those rocks in the few years since the discovery of the coast than anyone liked to remember. Spanish ships first, then British ships, and no survivors to tell the details to the navigators, so each voyage was as dangerous as the very first ones had been.

He hadn't expected it would be like that. But nothing had been as he had expected. He wondered if that meant a person wasn't supposed to expect anything, to just take each day as it came and hope nothing got any worse.

Life wasn't easy for an orphan boy in England. It had been terrible enough after his father left on a ship and didn't come back again. John could barely remember his father, barely remember standing on the dock with his mother, waving while the big wooden ship moved out to sea. His mother hadn't wept, but then, she never had. Even when she was sick and white-faced with pain, she hadn't cried. Sometimes John wanted to cry, but when that happened, he remembered his mother and how brave she had been, and he held back his tears.

And then, one day, she was dead, and the neighbours were making arrangements for the funeral, and looking at him pityingly. He knew there was only one place for an orphan. The workhouse. And John Richardson hadn't wanted to go to the workhouse. He'd heard too much about it, and nothing he had heard had been good. And so he ran from the house, ran from the sight of his mother, with her eyes shut and her hands folded, ran to the docks, knowing only that he did not want things to be the way they were; he wanted something better.

There were hungry days and cold, shivery nights, and he learned quickly to get out of the way of the deeply tanned men who toiled loading and unloading the ships that brought cargo from all over the world. If he wasn't fast enough there would be a sudden kick or a slap on the side of the head to send him sprawling.

Just when he thought he would have to give up and

go to the workhouse after all, everything changed. He was still asleep inside an empty barrel, and then suddenly there was a loud thump, a laugh, and his eyes jerked open, he tried to scramble free. But right in front of the barrel, two bare feet, and two strong legs, bare to the knee, and the laugh again. When the legs moved aside, John Richardson crawled out of the old barrel, frightened, hungry and defiant.

The sailor gave him some ship's biscuit and talked about far-off places John had never even heard of before, of sights too wonderful to be imagined, and then John walked with him to the ship, and before he even knew what was happening, he was signed on as cabin boy.

He wasn't sure any more what it was he had expected being cabin boy would mean, but whatever he had expected, nothing had been like that.

He had been so hungry when the sailor gave him the ship's biscuit that it had tasted more delicious than anything he could remember in a long time. And for the first few days, while the ship was still in port and it was still possible for people to sneak away, the food had been quite good. From the day they put out to sea, the food had got worse and worse until it was so bad only the sharp pangs of desperate hunger could force him to swallow it. There were bugs in all of it. In the flour, in the salted meat, in the sacks of dried beans, little black bugs and little white worms. And they got cooked up with everything else and, yes, eaten, because there was no time to pick them out, there were too many to pick out, and it was eat or starve, eat or die. And so John ate, gagging sometimes, but he ate.

He ate and he worked harder than he thought it was possible for a person to work and still stay alive.

Dzelarhons

He worked until he ached from head to foot and then, when he fell onto his hard pile of rags in a corner, he slept, until someone remembered there was something they wanted him to do, and kicked him awake, to go back to work again. If he didn't move quickly enough, or do the job well enough, he was slapped, kicked, even beaten, and made to do the job over again, quicker, better.

It wasn't what he had expected at all. They hadn't gone to the southern seas where the sun was warm and the trees full of brightly coloured birds. They hadn't gone where the scent of spice hung heavy in the air and the water was warm and clear under a turquoise sky. Nothing he had been told would happen had happened, and nobody had told him anything at all about this harsh coast, these threatening rocks, and the kind of storms that could toss a deck around so wildly all you wanted to do was get to the rail, hang on with both hands, and let the rotten food that had been supper come flying back up and out of you again.

He knew he had never been so miserable in all his life.

Everyone in the village was worried about Osprey Woman. Ever since her son had gone out in his dugout and not come back, Osprey Woman had been half mad with grief. Every morning she was awake and on the beach as the first light of the sun came up out of the sea. Standing in the cold water, she stretched her arms toward the huge red ball and sent her voice to the listening ear of the Creator. While the sleepies and dozies were still curled up in their beds, Osprey Woman was praying, certain her voice would be heard, for wasn't she the only one up so early, wasn't hers the only voice asking for help, and didn't the Creator always listen to prayers that came from the heart.

After her prayers were finished, she would walk along the beach, looking for her son. Months had passed since he had set out in his small dugout to gather gulls' eggs, and though they had found his cedar canoe smashed and broken on the rocks, they had never found his body. Until she saw with her own eyes that her son was dead, Osprey Woman believed him alive.

And so, every morning, she prayed for the sea to give up the great treasure it had taken from her. Every morning she prayed that her son be given back to her.

He had been soft and loving, he was laughter and joy, he was the light in her eyes and the song on her lips, and the ear of the Creator was open, she would surely be heard.

Osprey Woman finished her prayer, then bathed in the cold water, and when all her body glowed red with the cold, she pulled her clean tunic over her head and started her regular morning check of the shore. The raging storm that had held the coast in its grip for three days and nights had washed piles of sea weed onto the sand, huge logs, even trees, blown over by the wind, their roots like arms, hands, fingers washed clean by the rain and sea. Sometimes there were strange things for which Osprey Woman had no words or names, things washed from lands far across the heaving waters, lands the Pullers had even visited in the huge cedar dugouts, lands Osprey Woman would have liked to have seen for herself, but she had not been born to be a Puller, no matter how hard she had exercised, no matter how faithfully she had practiced, her arms and shoulders were just not big enough or strong enough to pull the paddle through the water well enough, or for a long enough time. And so she had been passed over and had to stay at home while others went out to visit the lands that formed the rim of the world. Osprey Woman stayed home, dreamed her dreams, wove her blankets, baskets, and tunics, and waited eagerly for the return of the travellers and the wonderful stories they brought home with them.

She had thought her son would be a Puller. He had the strong arms and shoulders that would be required, he could pull his paddle well, for long hours, without tiring, and he loved the stories as much as she did. And if the sea ever gave him back to her, he might still qualify.

And then she saw him. She wasn't surprised, she had expected all along that she would find him. She wasn't frightened, he was her son, and she had never had anything to fear from her son. She was just very relieved, and very happy.

She knelt, and brushed the bull kelp from his face,the sand from his skin, aand she sighed with relief when she saw the steady rise and fall of his shoulders. He was breathing. Her son was not dead.

But he was changed. Anyone who didn't know might even think this was a different boy all together. But Osprey Woman knew this was her son. She knew because she had faith. She knew because she had been praying at first and last light ever since he had failed to return. She had prayed that the sea give back her son, and so of course, this was her son, the sea had given him back. And if he was changed, what else could you expect after so long in the Kingdom Beneath The Waves.

His skin was much paler, but of course there is no sunlight in the kingdom beneath the sea. His hair was bleached from black to a light brown, but everyone knew salt water could do that to a person's hair. Everything about him was lighter, and smaller, but all you had to do was remember how the children looked in the summer time when they played in the waves all day and the skin on their hands and feet wrinkled and puckered, their palms and the soles of their feet startlingly pale against the deep tan of their bodies.

She lifted her son with only slight difficulty, and started walking back to the village, singing a song of thanks, praising the Creator, telling all the villagers her prayers had been answered and the sea had given back her son.

The villagers could hardly believe what they saw with their own eyes. Osprey Woman, smiling and happy, moving toward her house with a young boy in her arms. They hurried to help her, to offer her their congratulations, to join her in praising the Creator who had caused the sea to give back her son.

But when they saw the boy, they were stricken with doubt. The boy they remembered was much bigger, much stronger, older and darker, with hair like the raven's wing and deep rich brown skin. This boy didn't look like that at all, and when he opened his eyes, the people gasped, for his eyes were not quite as blue as the sky, not quite as gray as the sea. And his clothes, what was left of them, in no way at all resembled the clothing of the people. In fact, in many ways, the shreds of cloth reminded them of the clothes worn by the Strangers, except the Strangers' clothes were much more beautiful and impressive. This boy was nearly naked. It was all a great puzzle

81

to the people.

Almost as great a puzzle as the Strangers. For more generations than anyone except the Memorizers could remember, there had been only the people on the island. Sometimes the Pullers headed off across the water to visit the countries weeks and even months away, but the people who lived in those countries looked very much like the people of the island. Black hair, black eyes, brown skin, bearing witness to the common maternity of all people, proving they were all the children of Copper Woman, all cousins, if not brothers and sisters. And then the Strangers came, looking nothing at all like any of the people, some of them with hair like the sun, some with hair like dry grass, some with hair the colour of sand, and eyes of all shades of blue, gray, green, brown and black. And now this boy, with strange coloured eyes and pale skin, whose shreds of clothing were very faintly reminiscent of the elegant uniforms of the People Who Live On The Great Boats. But all of those people were men, with hairy bodies and faces, who carried weapons and were quick to use them, and this was certainly no man, this was most certainly a boy, and Osprey Woman said it was her son. And who would know better than a mother whether or not a child was hers? And so they put away their doubts, and accepted what Osprey Woman told them. Her son had been taken by the seas, had spent long weeks in the Undersea Kingdom, and had been returned to her, bleached and altered, because the Creator had heard her prayers and had rewarded her faith.

John Richardson stirred weakly, his body protesting, his muscles aching, his head pounding. He remembered the storm, he remembered leaning over the side of the ship, sick and dizzy. He remembered the huge wall of gray water that slammed against the side of the ship and pulled his hands loose, sweeping him overboard. He remembered struggling frantically, his calls for help lost in the howling of the wind, and then he remembered only confused images, a large floating log, bare branches he could grab, and the steady pounding of angry water against his body.

He opened his eyes. A woman was smiling down on him, her hand soft against his cheek. He tried to speak, but his voice was caught in his throat, and then the woman was holding a wooden bowl of something hot against his lips. He drank and the warmth filled his belly, his eyes fluttered, and he went back to sleep.

Everyone had heard the sound the boy had made, and if any of them had any lingering doubt that this was Osprey Woman's son, that doubt evaporated. The boy had made a sound exactly like the call of a gull. What other sound would you expect from a boy who had spent so long in the Undersea Kingdom?

The next time John Richardson wakened, he was lying naked in a bed of otter skins. He was warm, he was comfortable, and as soon as his eyes opened, the smiling woman lifted his head and began to spoon warm soup into his mouth. He ate eagerly, smiling at the woman, who talked softly to him in a language he didn't understand, a language unlike anything he had ever heard, a language full of little clicks and sounds he knew he would have trouble learning to make. When he spoke to her in his own language she just stared at him, then a look of puzzlement and pity crossed her face, tears came to her eyes and she looked so forlorn he reached out his hand and patted her face reassuringly. The sadness vanished from her kind face, she smiled and then he was being held close, the way his mother had held him when he was little, and he was rocked and cradled until his eyes closed, and he slept again.

Within a few days, John Richardson was able to walk without needing to hold onto the strong arm of his new mother. Everywhere he went, people smiled at him and offered him food. Children ran up to him, staring openly, and when he spoke to them, their eyes grew wide, but not fearful. The Carvers showed him their work, the Spinners and Weavers smiled and invited him to try to duplicate their expert movements. The Pullers let him hold a paddle, and when he didn't know how to hold it or how to move it, they looked sad, spoke to him gently, corrected his grip and demonstrated again and again how to move his arms and shoulders.

He learned the words for food and drink, he learned the words for fire and wood, he learned the words for bowl and spoon, for paddle and dugout, for warm and cold, and he learned the word for mother.

The first time he called Osprey Woman his mother, she wept with happiness and held him close, stroking his face, smoothing his hair and smiling through her tears. And when she went to the shore to greet the new day and sing her thanks to the Creator, he went with her, stood in the water with her, and copied the movements she made with her hands and arms.

All the people watched, and were pleased. Every day there was proof that Osprey Woman had been right from the beginning; this was indeed her son.

His sojourn in the Undersea Kingdom had done more than shrink him, done more than alter him physically. Much of what he had known before the accident had been washed from his memory, but that was only to be expected, everyone knew when a person went from one reality to another, everything, including the person, changed.

One day, John Richardson learned the word "Ta-Naz," the word for "boy." He liked the sound. It jumped from his tongue like a small frog jumping from a rock, it flew through the air like a hummingbird. It would, he decided, make a fine new name for his new life. He began calling himself Ta-Naz, which was not really a name, but it became one when he took it for his own. Soon everyone called him Ta-Naz, and he almost forgot he had once had another name, another mother, another life, in another land and culture.

He had never been so happy. Every day his life was more wonderful than it had been the day before. And every morning he went with his mother to thank the Creator for bringing him from death to a full, rich life.

Ta-Naz knew he would never be able to go after the huge whales, harpoon ready, singing the song of the whaler. He knew he would never qualify to be a Puller and to travel to distant lands; his skill with a dugout was simply not good enough. Already, boys much younger than he could paddle more smoothly for longer periods of time. But Ta-Naz wasn't jealous; there were so many other things he could do, so many other things he could become, things he could enjoy.

He enjoyed going out in the small cedar dugout to catch cod and salmon. He enjoyed digging for clams, or picking oysters and mussels from the rocks. He enjoyed diving for sea urchins, or going out to the wiers to harvest fish and crabs. He enjoyed helping harvest and dry the nutritious sea weed, going into the woods searching for edible roots and tubers. He enjoyed picking salmonberries in the spring time and huckleberries and blackberries in the summer time. Every day there was something to do, food to gather and preserve, games to play, things to learn, and all the adults seemed to enjoy teaching him whatever he needed to learn.

Ta-Naz especially enjoyed sitting with a carved wooden comb, carefully combing the fur of the small white dogs that lived in the houses with the people. The dogs were spoiled, pampered, and carefully tended, their long slinky fur treasured. The Spinners would carefully save the fur Ta-Naz removed from the comb, then, expertly and patiently, they would spin it into fibre for the Weavers to work into their capes and blankets. The little white dogs stood patiently, tails wagging, while the boy gently and carefully combed their fur, saving the strands of hair, laying them in a clean basket, and Ta-Naz found the work calming and pleasant. It gave him a chance to think of all the new words and skills he was learning, and, increasingly, as he combed, he sang songs of his own composition, songs in his new language.

Osprey Woman listened to the happy sound of her son singing, and knew it didn't matter to her that he would never become a Puller, never travel as she had so often longed to do. Ta-Naz had already travelled further than most people, most Pullers, ever get a chance to travel. Ta-Naz had travelled to the Undersea Kingdom, and come back to her. He had travelled to death and come back to life, and that was voyage enough for anybody.

The villagers, listening to the sound of Ta-Naz singing, smiled to themselves. Every day the boy learned more of what he had forgotten in the Undersea Kingdom. His pronunciation improved, and he had almost lost the strange accent he had once had when he tried to speak the language he had forgotten. Everyone was very glad Ta-Naz had come back to live with them. He was growing stronger every day, and if his skill with a dugout was less than it ought to have been, perhaps that only meant that he was supposed to spend most of his life on the land, now that he had so completely explored the sea. His skin was darker than it had been, but still much lighter than anybody else's, and the people realized that for the rest of his life he would carry this mark of the time he had spent lost in the water.

And then, several years after Ta-Naz had returned from the Undersea Kingdom, the huge wooden boat of the Strangers appeared on the horizon. The people went down to the beach to stare in wonder at the tall masts, the furled sails. When they saw the strange dugout coming toward them, they waved welcome, and threw the soft down from the breast of waterfowl on the waves to welcome the Strangers.

Nobody noticed Ta-Naz move away from the welcoming throng. Nobody noticed him as he went to the house he and his mother shared with three other families. They were all too busy welcoming the strangers.

The Strangers had beads, blankets, knives, and metal kettles they wanted to trade for seal and otter skins. The Strangers needed fresh water and wanted permission to cut tall trees to make new masts for their ship. The people made presents of fresh and smoked fish, of oysters, clams, and venison.

And Ta-Naz stayed away from everything that was happening. His mother asked him what was wrong, and he just shook his head and walked away, and those who saw it began to wonder.

And then, one day, unexpectedly, Ta-Naz was seen by one of the Strangers. The man pointed, his face registering shock, and from his mouth came a loud sound that made Ta-Naz jump with fear and race for the woods. The Stranger whirled and ran to where the officers were seated on the beach, supervising the loading of supplies. When the Stranger blurted out what he had seen, there was great excitement, and then several Strangers ran for the bush, chasing after Ta-Naz.

It wasn't easy to understand what it was that had the Strangers so excited. But, finally, several of the men went into the bush and came back hours later, with Ta-Naz. The boy stood defiantly, glaring angrily at the Strangers, who pointed excitedly at him, and talked eagerly among themselves.

"That boy," the chief of the Strangers pointed at Ta-Naz, "That boy is my cabin boy, John Richardson. You must return him to me."

"That," Osprey Woman said quietly, "is not true. He is my son."

"He is my cabin boy!" the captain argued.

"No," Osprey Woman said firmly.

"If you don't return my cabin boy to me," the officer threatened angrily, "I will use the big guns on my ship to blow this village to pieces."

The warriors stirred uneasily. They had given nothing but friendship to the Strangers, and now they were being threatened. They moved in a semi-circle, their weapons ready. The Strangers looked at the warriors and glanced uneasily at their angry captain. The big guns were out in the bay, on the ship, and if the warriors got angry, few, if any, of the Strangers would make it back to the ship alive.

"Calm yourself," one of the sub-chiefs said firmly. "We will go to the Queen Mother, and ask her what to do about this."

Ta-Naz had seen the Queen Mother many times. He had seen her walking with her daughters, talking to the people, asking them what they felt was needed, or wanted, to improve life for all. He had seen her laughing with her grandchildren, joining them in their games and their play. He had seen her walking with her son, the Chief, instructing him in his duties, listening to his thoughts and ideas, his plans and his hopes.

He had never before seen her in the full official regalia of the Queen Mother.

The Queen Mother stood quietly, her gentle black eyes watching closely the faces and reactions of those involved in the disagreement.

"This boy," the Captain of the Strangers said firmly, "is my cabin boy. His name is John Richardson. I demand you return him to me."

"Everyone knows," Osprey Woman said equally firmly, "Ta-Naz is my son. He was taken by the sea, he journeyed to the Kingdom Beneath The Sea, and the Creator sent him back to me."

"Ta-Naz," the Queen Mother demanded. "Do you understand what the Stranger is saying?"

"Yes Queen Mother," Ta-Naz answered honestly. "He is the captain of the ship. He is the Chief of those Strangers."

"And you understand his speech?"

"Yes, Queen Mother."

"And do you wish to go with him?"

"No, Queen Mother," Ta-Naz said quietly.

"Are you certain?" The Queen Mother looked deeply into his eyes, her face serious. "This decision will affect you for the rest of your life."

"Queen Mother," Ta-Naz said, tears filling his eyes. "I was hungry, I lived less pleasantly than our dogs do. I will not go back. I will not be a slave, and a cabin boy is a slave. I would rather," he said quietly, "return to the Undersea Kingdom, and if I am forced to go back to the Strangers and their ship, I will jump from the deck and sink like a stone."

The Queen Mother looked at him and nodded gently.

"You are to translate my words for the Chief of the Strangers," the Queen Mother commanded. Ta-Naz nodded, then moved to stand near his mother, Osprey Woman, looking across a space of floor to the Captain.

"Tell the Chief of the Strangers your name," the Queen Mother said.

"My name is Ta-Naz," he said.

"Your name is John Richardson!" the Captain thundered.

"My name," he repeated, "is Ta-Naz."

"Who is your mother?" the Queen Mother demanded.

"Osprey Woman is my mother," Ta-Naz answered, and smiled up at the woman who had saved his life.

"Your mother is dead!" the Captain argued. "You are my cabin boy."

"No, Queen Mother," Osprey Woman laughed. "I am not dead."

"And who is that boy standing beside you?"

"He is my son," Osprey Woman answered.

"Ta-Naz." The Queen Mother's smile faded. "Who is your mother?"

"Osprey Woman is my mother," Ta-Naz repeated. "I am her son."

The Queen Mother looked at Ta-Naz, then at Osprey Woman, and finally at the Strangers and their Captain.

"Tell the Chief of the Strangers," she said quietly, "that he must not threaten me, my son, this village, or any of the people who live here. Tell him if he threatens us, or makes a move against us, we will send Pullers to all our friends in the villages of this coast. We will send Pullers to our friends in the villages of the countries on the other side of the water. We will meet his force with an army so big he will not be able to count the numbers moving against him."

The Captain listened to what Ta-Naz translated, then flicked his eyes at his crewmen. They were outnumbered, and the young Chief stood with his war club in his hands, ready to do whatever his mother told him. The Captain dropped his eyes, and nodded briefly.

"Osprey Woman says this is her son. How could a mother make a mistake about something as important as that? A mother gives life to a child, and we are all convinced Osprey Woman did, in fact, give life back to Ta-Naz." And the Queen Mother smiled at the woman. "Ta-Naz says Osprey Woman is his mother. A child knows who it is who cares for him when he is ill, feeds him, clothes him, and loves him. A child knows his mother. You say this boy is yours, and the boy says no. How could a woman of this village have a Stranger for a son? How could a Stranger have a woman of this village for a mother?"

The Captain stared at the Queen Mother, and his face told her he knew and understand her decision.

"If one of our dogs," she laughed, "had her puppy in my bed, that would not make that puppy a member of the Royal Family. But if my grandson were born on your boat, he would still be my grandson." The Captain nodded, and tried to hide his anger. "Ta-Naz," the Queen Mother said firmly, "is the son of Osprey Woman. He is one of us, and we will fight, if need be, to protect him and keep him with us." And the Queen Mother walked away with her daughters.

Ta-Naz stood in the chill water of the sea with Osprey Woman standing beside him, and as the sun rose for the start of a new day, they sent their prayers of thanks to the listening ear of the Creator. And as his voice rose to the skies, Ta-Naz knew he had never been happier, never felt more blessed, and he promised the Creator that he would spend his life well, and never forget to express his gratitude to his people, to his mother, Osprey Woman, and to that one who is in charge of all the affairs of the world.

LAZY BOY

There was a time, long ago, when the world was not shaped as it is now. At that time there was only one huge flat piece of earth, floating in one huge ocean, and the ball that is the world was carefully fitted into its own hole in the blanket that is the sky.

At that time, Spider Woman lived in a land far to the south, a land with little rain, a land of strange beauty where people walked on sand and under a sky that seldom knew rain.

Spider Woman lived under the sand, in a huge web she had spun herself, and her children lived with her, listening to the happy sound of the lambs' hooves on their roof.

And then the earth began to shudder and quake, to split and crack, and Vancouver Island broke loose from the mainland and floated off, and sisters and brothers waved goodbye to each other sadly.

The world had begun to slip from its proper hole.

And through the gaps in the hole in the sky, the Birds of Torment began to appear. Until this time, the people had known no pain, no sorrow, and no discomfort, for the Birds of Torment were unable to get past the world, but as the world began to slip, the birds edged and inched through, and the people began to suffer terribly and cry bitterly.

Spider Woman heard the weeping. She left her many children in charge of her affairs, and climbed up the silver web-strand that leads to her house.

Spider Woman began to weave a net of silver around the slipping world, shooting strands of her webbing up to the moon, twisting and knotting the magic pattern that only she has ever been able to weave, and then she climbed up her own web-rope and stood on the moon, heaving and tugging, her sturdy little body straining and sweating.

When the world was almost in place again, Spider Woman took a section of rainbow and straightened it carefully, then wove a simple basket and fastened it to the end, and with this, the first Lacrosse stick, she caught the Birds of Torment as they flew through the sky, and one by one she stuffed them back through the hole to the place where they belonged.

The only ones she couldn't catch and force back into their proper place were the ones that brought toothache, earache, headache and stomachache.

Then Spider Woman pushed the earth into its proper place, and tied the ends of her web securely. Some nights, when the moon is full and the clouds rolled away, you can see the Spider Woman's web still cradling our world and holding us safe.

Then Spider Woman went to the tallest tree in all

the world and explained her concerns. The tree willingly offered herself, and became the pole Spider Woman placed under the earth to keep it steady.

To this very day you can see silver webs in the branches of trees, as the children of Spider Woman and the children of the big tree help each other; the trees provide a home for the spiders, the spiders catch the bugs that otherwise might infest and destroy the tree. When you see them, remember how the trees and spiders worked together to make this world a safe place for you to live.

When the world was safe, Spider Woman went back to her own land and the home she had fashioned under the sand, and she lived with her children where she could hear the patter of lambs' hooves on her roof, hear the sound of the flute the sheep herders played, hear the songs and laughter of the women as they wove the wool into blankets and rugs.

Life began to be pleasant again. The people got used to the new shape of the earth, and Old Man, whose beard is so long that sometimes you can see it twisting between the rocks and trees on the shore, watched over the pole that held the world in place, and Time did what it has always done, and passed as steadily as possible.

And then, one day, a baby boy was found on the beach. An ordinary enough looking baby boy with no distinguishing marks or tattoos on his body. The people who found him supposed he was the son of fishing people who had been dropped under the waves when their dugout capsized, or maybe even dragged under by a blackfish or a huge halibut.

They knew that Orca, who feeds her own babies with milk from her breasts, as do women, would have heard the little boy crying, and because there is a link between Orca and the milk-drinking children of women, she would have delivered the orphan child to the edge of the water near the village.

Orca has always been a friend to people; but people have not always been friendly towards Orca, nor have we been as considerate of her children as she has been of ours.

The people dried the salt spray from the chubby body of the orphan baby and fed him small pieces of baked fish, some lily root baked in ashes and chewed soft by the older women, and they gave him sips of nettle-leaf tea, which he sucked from the edge of a small thin bowl. He burped and laughed, waved his baby arms and legs happily, and went to sleep.

He wakened only when he was hungry, and the people fed him willingly, even though years passed and he grew bigger and bigger and hungrier and hungrier and larger and larger until he was twice the size of a grown man.

Four times a day the giant would waken and ask for food, and four times a day the people would feed him, he would smile, thank them, then go back to sleep again.

Everyone called him Lazy Boy and wondered if the day would ever come when he would do some work and begin to justify his existence.

One day Old Man coughed, and the pole holding the world in place trembled. Then the creeks and even the rivers began to overflow their banks, the tide came in and kept on coming, and the lakes moved down to join the sea.

The people gathered the elderly and the infants in

their arms and ran for safety, yelling at Lazy Boy to get up, to flee, and when he didn't, some of the strong young people ran back and tried to rouse him, but he continued snoring.

They tried to lift him and carry him, but he was too big and too heavy.

"He'll wake up," they assured each other hopefully, "as soon as the water gets in his ears. Nobody can sleep with water in his ears," and they ran to save their own lives.

Sure enough, as the water entered his ears, Lazy Boy woke up and realized immediately what had happened. To the total amazement of his foster sisters, foster brothers, and foster parents, he stood up, taller and taller and taller, stretching himself until the clouds surrounded his head like a helmet. He raised his arms, spread his fingers, and from his mouth a sound issued unlike anything heard since Tem Eyos Ki sang her song, and the surface of the water quivered.

He sang again and the channels of the rivers deepened, the basins of the lakes sank, the water began to recede to fill the holes, leaving fish stranded in the bottom branches of the trees, hanging like fruit, food to replace what the people lost when the smokehouses were flooded.

Then Lazy Boy shrank down to his normal size, which was still huge, and he lay down and went back to sleep.

The people returned to their villages, and four times a day they willingly fed the dozy giant who smiled sleepily and often yawned contentedly, even while accepting the food the people prepared.

Then the trees started growing closer and closer to the village, moving down the hillsides, pushing nearer, threatening to shove the very houses into the chuck, and it was the sound of axes clanging desperately that wakened the huge boy sleeping in the sun.

He watched for a few moments, rubbing his eyes in puzzlement. Everyone who could was fighting the trees, even little children had sharp sticks or bone knives, sawing and slashing frantically at elderberry and fir, cedar and pine, alder and aspen, even at the sacred redclothed arbutus that combines the characteristics of both kinds of trees, having leaves like deciduous, but not losing them all in the fall, staying green through the winter like the conifers.

Lazy Boy rolled himself in a ball, as if he were frightened, then he started to roll around the periphery of the village, uprooting the trees and piling them together neatly, weaving them into a big fence, and when he had cleared even more space than there had been before the trees went berserk, when everything was neat again, he rolled back to his favourite sleeping place and curled comfortably on his side, smiling as he dozed.

The people hadn't yet recovered from their amazement when the most marvelous of all marvels began to happen, a thing so wonderful it is called, simply, The Glory.

A bright light began to glow on the surface of the sea. Flashing like the scales of Sisiutl, the magic sea serpent, bright scarlet, sharp yellow, blue as a dragonfly, green as the outer shell of the June beetle, shimmering and glowing, flashing and sparkling, closer and closer The Glory came until the air began to tremble, and the earth quiver with the vibrations of the colours.

A young girl who had been unable to hear the

sounds of voices put her hands over her eyes and fell to her knees, her head shaking violently as the tremors of colour pounded the bones that grew across her ear canals, powdering them, and she was the first to hear the sound the glowing paddles made as they sliced the sea.

Lazy Boy leaped to his feet and stretched his massive arms towards the glow, tears of joy coursing down his cheeks and landing on the grass, where they turned into tiny strawberries.

The gigantic dugout scraped onto the beach and three very old men dressed in beauty stepped out, the colours flashing on their capes and kilts, and each of these ancients was nearly as tall as Lazy Boy himself.

The people trembled in fear, and only the girl who had once been deaf dared to smile and step forward, hands outstretched in peace, thanking the Supernatural Uncles for their gift to her, the gift of birdsong, the gift of the sound of the wind high in the green trees, the gift so many of us take for granted.

"Thank you," she said, hearing the sound of her own voice for the first time.

"Thank you," Lazy Boy said, a voice as beautiful as that of Loon before her neck was stretched and her song silenced. "You have protected me in my helplessness and fed me in my hunger. You have kept me warm and given me drink when I thirsted. Without your love, I would have died, and there would have been nobody to replace my fourth uncle when he became too old to continue his work. My fourth uncle is Old Man who holds the world in place at the end of a long pole, and now his brothers have come to take me to him so that I can continue the work and he can retire and enjoy his old age." And the people knew that if they had not cared for the baby Orca had delivered to their beach, this day would have been the day the world ended.

Lazy Boy walked to the dugout, got in, and lifted a golden paddle. His three ancient Supernatural Uncles climbed in with him and the magic craft took off for the other world.

There was a moment when the pole was transferred from the old back to the strong young back, a moment when the earth shifted and the bird of menstrual cramps squeezed through the hole, but Frog Woman taught us the kneeling position to defeat the cramps, so the bird was thwarted.

Sometimes, even today, the earth shifts and trembles. This happens when Lazy Boy hears a joke and his giggles make his shoulders move.

DZELARHONS

I

In those days there were no people here, and no islands, either. The huge bulk of the continent stretched uncharted, covered with trees and mountains, bright with rivers and lakes, and there were animals and birds, fish and insects, flowers and all things, except people and islands. The sun rose as it always had, and warmed the earth. It travelled across the expanse of this part of the world, and fell to sleep beyond the rim of the sea. It is said that this enormous mass of land lay balanced on the back of Frog Woman, who slept in the water, and whose breathing caused the waves which lapped on the shore. And it is said that one day, in her sleep, Frog Woman coughed, and the edges of the world as it was then, crumbled, and the first small islands floated away from the main body of land, and nestled themselves in the warm current we now call the Japanese Current, and on those islands in those days lived only the animals and birds.

The sun warmed the islands as it had warmed the main body of land, and the fierce storms that lashed in from the sea battered the islands, bent the trees into gnarled shapes, and brought drenching rains. And with these storms, so long ago nobody can say when, came the first of the round, hide-bottomed coracles, and with it, the first people. And the only one of those people who survived on that small island, was the one who was a child when she arrived, the one who lived for a time in a cave near the shore, then came from the cave and built for herself a small house, built of rocks and logs, built of branches and sod. The one who fed herself from the richness of the sea, fed herself with oysters and clams, with mussels and crabs, with oolichan and herring and cod. The one who was the first mother, who first made the marks still to be seen carved into the rocks of the coast, the one who patiently, for more years than any of us will live, rubbed with a sharp-pointed rock against sandstone and granite, leaving the evidence of her visions, leaving messages we no longer know how to read or understand.

And this first mother was Copper Woman, and her children and grandchildren were many, and from them come all the people of the earth, all the men and all the women, all the children are come from this first mother, and are cousins, whatever their colour.

When Copper Woman had been living for many generations, and her children were many, it happened that Frog Woman again coughed, and the coughing caused the waves to splash, some water went up her nose, and she sneezed. It was a monstrous sneeze, and it shook Frog Woman awake.

The edges of the large shelf were again crumbling, and drifting away, only this time, because the sneeze had been greater than that first cough which broke loose the small islands, the pieces floating away were larger. And one of the pieces was so big it was almost a world unto itself, and is today called Vancouver Island. And you can still see the outline on the mainland where the Island used to fit in and be all of one part, although it will never again be joined to that big shelf.

And there were children standing on the shore, weeping, and watching their parents drifting off on the separated island, and parents standing on the shore watching their children drift toward where the sun goes when she goes to sleep. Sisters waved goodbye to brothers, and brothers waved goodbye to sisters. Nieces and nephews watched aunts and uncles ride the separating island, and some even jumped into the water to try to swim to the other, that they not be separated forever. Frog Woman was so amazed by everything that had happened that she split her skin into millions of little pieces and each piece became a frog, smaller than Frog Woman had ever been, and some of the frogs swam after the separating islands, to be with the people and to try to make the people less sad, to cheer the people with the sound of their song, and make the people laugh each time they saw the wide smile on the face of the frogs.

But some of the islands had already drifted too far away for the frogs to be able to catch up and so it is there are islands to the north where the people have never seen a live frog, and yet have drawings and carvings of Frog Woman, for the first exiles remembered the brave little creatures which had tried to swim after them, be with them, and help them. And because the little frogs had proven themselves to be courageous and loyal, the figures, carvings, and drawings these northern people made were used as symbols of bravery and determination. In time, the people tried to train themselves to be like the frogs in those things, even though they had been gone on those lost islands for so long they had not seen a living frog.

One year followed another, and the children were living in all their separated places, and one generation grew old and another took its place. Some of the families could visit back and forth across the open water, could load a dugout with food and supplies and paddle from their own village to one of the islands where their brothers and sisters, aunts and uncles lived. But few people even knew where the northern islands were, and of those who knew even fewer could manage to visit. Far to the west, in the direction where the sun goes when she sleeps, were more people, on other islands, people who had drifted so far their own cousins had forgotten them.

And still the children prospered and the numbers of people grew. And Copper Woman, who had lived more years than we could count, was still alive. And the years passed, and on those islands far to the west the people spoke often of the place where the sun rises, and of how much they missed the relatives they had been forced to leave behind, and of their dear mother and grandmother, Copper Woman, whom they still loved and missed.

And so it was in that western place, the bravest and most daring of the people decided to come back, to defy the expanse of water, to put sails on the dugouts, and to attach outriggers, from which they suspended baskets of shellfish packed in sea weed. Riding the winds of the storms, they journeyed back toward the land of their origin, a land they had never seen but which their grandparents and great-grandparents had told them existed, a land they called sometimes Wu Feng and sometimes Li Sehms and which we have sometimes called Temlehan and sometimes called Eden, and even called other names, and all those names can be translated as meaning "Paradise" or "Blessed Lands" or "Place of Peace and Plenty."

Though the people here had forgotten those few who had been on the lands which drifted westward, the ones who had no choice but to watch helplessly as they were taken away from their home had never forgotten. And one of these women had a daughter which she named in honour of that first mother, and the child was called Dzelarhons, and though an infant, was taken by her parents when they set off with the others in search of Li Sehms.

The trip across the seas was long and bitter, and many of those who had set out in that other land never made it to the place of their dreams. Their bodies were lowered into the cold water and left floating, faces turned to the sky, the tears of the survivors mixing with the ocean which washes, even today, upon our rocks and shores. But still they headed toward the birthplace of the sun, and when there was no wind to fill the sails, the men and women took up their paddles and pulled, some by day and some by night, pulling in sun or rain, by moon or star, heading always towards the land where their first mother lived. And when they were cold or hungry, when they were tired or lonely, they sang, and the child Dzelarhons sang with them.

From the time she was old enough to understand, Dzelarhons worked at the tasks she could to help in the bitter voyage. She scooped water from the ocean and poured it over the clams and oysters in the baskets, that they might filter it and get their food from it. Whenever the dugouts passed through a bed of sea weed or kelp, Dzelarhons helped pull fresh weed from the sea and put it in the baskets to feed the shelled creatures. She sat with a fishing line in her hand, trolling for any kind of fish which might be tempted to swallow the hook, and when the sun beat down fiercely, it was Dzelarhons who would take the woven hats of the people and soak them in salt water, then replace them on the sweating heads, to cool them and strengthen them in their work.

A day came when they sighted land, and everyone celebrated, some wept tears of joy and some confessed that they had doubted they would ever find Paradise. The dugouts were battered, the sails frayed and almost useless, and all the people were so tired they thought they would never in their lives get enough rest. And when they came upon a quiet place, where they could beach the dugouts safely, they landed, and said, "Our journey is over, we are arrived."

The baskets of shellfish were emptied into the clean water of the new place, and the people threw nets from the rocks and trapped fish for their first meal, and from the trees they gathered fruit, and for the first time in who knows how long, they had enough to eat, and slept free of the spray of splashing waves.

And they stayed there, and Dzelarhons grew to womanhood and married with one of the young men, and she had children, and they grew to adulthood and married with other young men and women of those people, and a granddaughter was born, and to her, Dzelarhons gave her name, and that child grew to adulthood and married, and so it went for a time.

And the people began to realize that they had not arrived at Paradise at all, for there was no sign of their first mother here, no sign of Copper Woman, and no other people except themselves on the island, and while most of them were satisfied and happy, a few still grieved and dreamed of returning to Li Sehms. Finally, the day came when they again packed their goods in their dugouts, and the bravest of them set out to again search for the place where the sun is born, and one of the people who set out on the search was a young woman named Dzelarhons, and on her head she wore a woven hat like the ones worn by those first searchers, a conical hat with a wide brim, and the cone flared out to a flat top, and on that flat top, because it pleased her and because it had been carved by a friend, Dzelarhons fastened a wooden carving of a frog.

As before, the sails filled with wind and when the wind rested, the people pulled the paddles, and the craft moved across the water, toward the place where they saw the sun rise in the morning, and though many dugouts set out in search of the homeland, the fierce storms dispersed them, and some of the dugouts were scattered, as the fractured pieces of the world had been scattered, and the people in those crafts were, again, cut off from family, and forced to find their own way in a huge world they did not know.

Under hot sun or chill wind, pelted by rain and

often burning with thirst, still the many times great-grandchildren of Copper Woman directed their dugouts towards the birthplace of the daylight, and finally, after many dangers and much bitterness, they again arrived at land. And this time there were people living in that land, and these people had never seen a living frog, but had some carvings of the frog, and when they saw the little figure on Dzelarhons' hat, they recognized it and made the newcomers welcome, even though these people were of the GrizzlyBear people, and quite fearsome and powerful, as is the Grizzlybear.

The sea people who had travelled so far to meet these GrizzlyBear people were shocked and disappointed to discover they shared no common language, only a few words which sounded the same but seemed to mean different things. In trying to tell the GrizzlyBear people that they had come from the sea a confusion was caused, and this confusion made the GrizzlyBear people think the newcomers had come from the depths of the sea, and again, when the sea people tried to describe themselves as fishing people, the GrizzlyBear people misunderstood and so it was they called the newcomers Salmon people, or Salmon-Eater people.

The GrizzlyBear people had a social system centred on inheritance through the mother, and the paramount woman was called the Mother, or the Mother Of All, or sometimes White Haired Woman, or sometimes Old Woman, or Grandmother, or Crone. She passed her position and wealth, her powers, songs, stories, and all that is important, to her daughters, and the oldest of her daughters would, in turn, be the Mother, or queen. All children were raised by the women for the first years of their lives, and then, some time between six and eight years, the boys went to live with their uncles, the brothers of the mothers, and from the uncles, the boys learned how to be men, and how to do the things usually done by men. And so it was that living with the headman or chief of the GrizzlyBear people's hunting party was a nephew, who saw Dzelarhons and wanted to marry her. He expected from the unusual hat she wore, and from the carving of the frog decorating it, that Dzelarhons would be at least a princess, and maybe even a queen, and that marrying with her would mean his children, too, would be rulers.

And so it was arranged, and the people from across the sea had reason to celebrate, and as this was to be the first wedding in the new land, all the newcomers worked to make it memorable. They made for Dzelarhons trousers, or pants of soft tanned leather, and they made her four shirts or coats or robes, to be worn over the pants, and one was a shirt of soft tanned leather decorated with dentalia shells, and another was made from the bellyfur of the young sea otter. One of the shirts was wide and long, down to the knees, and was made of the fur from the back of the adult sea otter, and the fourth was a heavy parka for winter, made of two layers of soft fur, the outside one water repellent, the inside layer turned so the fur touched her skin and would keep her warm no matter how hard the wind blew, how cold the rain or snow that fell.

They caught and smoked fish, picked baskets of oysters, dug baskets of clams, and prepared food for everyone. Then they cut planks from a tree and laid them across two fine dugouts, and loaded all the food on the planks, and Dzelarhons stood amidst this plenty wearing her leather pants and her leather shirt decorated with dentalia shell. All the people from across the sea travelled with her, and they moved in a flotilla across the bay to where the GrizzlyBear people lived.

Dzelarhons did not know her intended bridegroom very well, but she was content with the idea of marrying him. She had been too long without a proper home, too long isolated with just the same few people, and had watched helplessly as so many of her cousins and friends had been blown off course by the howling winds. She hoped to find peace and security, she hoped to find love and friendship and a sense of belonging so that her children would not need to roam as she had roamed all her life.

The GrizzlyBear people met the newcomers on the beach and they spread waterfowl down on the water as a sign of peace, and eagle down as a sign of respect, and the newcomers sang songs of greeting. All the people helped unload the food from the dugouts, and when they saw the clothes her family had made for her, they praised Dzelarhons and her people, and escorted her to the house of the bridegroom, and her mother and her aunts made a couch for the couple, and made it by spreading warm robes of otter and seal on the floor. Then everyone feasted and sang, and the bridegroom was proud and drank the fermented beer his uncle provided everyone, and the nephew laughed often and danced.

And when it was time, Dzelarhons was escorted to her marriage bed by her female relatives, and she sat on the bed of furs and they brushed her hair until it shone, and decorated it with ermine skin and waterfowl down, and made her look beautiful.

___

When the bridegroom entered, the female attendants and relatives left the house, and Dzelarhons was alone, for the first time, with her husband. She smiled at him, and he moved to the bed of furs and sat down on it, staring at her. Outside, she could hear the people dancing and singing and feasting and celebrating, but inside there was only the sound of two people breathing softly. Then the bridegroom laughed contentedly, and got up from the bed, and moved to a pile of torches, selected one, and brought it back to the fire. He lit the end of the torch, then handed it to Dzelarhons. "Here," he said. "You are my wife now, and it is your job to hold this torch over me while I sleep, so that the mosquitoes and black flies not nip me and disturb my sleep." And he lay down on the bed of furs her family and friends had made. "Move over," he said, "you are in my way," and he kicked with his feet, so she moved off the bed and sat holding the burning torch, wondering what strange manner of wedding night this was and if it was the custom of the GrizzlyBear people or only some idea the young man had found in the fermented beer.

Twice she lowered the torch, and twice when she did this the young bridegroom awakened and yelled at her, and cursed her for a lazy woman, and told her she was his wife now, and would have to do as he said, and have to live as did his people, and guard the flame and keep the torch burning, and if she did not do it properly, he would teach her a lesson. And Dzelarhons wondered at that, as well, but she wanted to behave in a seemly way, and be a good wife, and raise her family in harmony, and so she resigned herself to guarding this torch while the drunken young man slept.

Dzelarhons

The torch burned lower and lower and soon the
heat of it began to scorch her hand, and she lifted
part of her beautiful leather shirt decorated with
dentalia, and wrapped that around her hand, to
protect her from the heat. Outside, she could hear
her people leaving and knew they would be gone for
four nights, leaving her alone with her bridegroom,
and when they returned, as was their custom, they
would bring more food, and more furs, and would
celebrate for days, and if she decided in that time
she did not want to live here with this young man,
she could return with her family. And so, though she
could smell her beautiful shirt scorching in the heat
of the torch, Dzelarhons waited, and told herself she
would try hard to be the wife this young man seemed
to want.

Her eyelids grew heavy and her body begged for
sleep, but there was this torch to be considered and
besides, the sodden young man was sprawled across
the entire bed and there was no room for her. So she
sat, holding the dying torch, and when the torch was
reduced to ashes, she pulled her scorched and
ruined shirt over her head, spread it out on the floor,
and lay down on it and went to sleep.

Nobody came to the house of the newlyweds, the
entire village of GrizzlyBear people stayed away, to
give the young people privacy and a chance to get to
know each other, and so nobody saw, at first, how
the young man treated Dzelarhons. He wakened
before her, his head aching from the fermented beer,
and when he saw her sleeping next to the burned-out
torch, he became angry, and jumped up from the bed
of furs, and kicked her in the ribs, and shook her
awake, and shouted at her. "You fool of a foreigner,
see, you have let the torch go out!" "And what was I
to do," Dzelarhons said, "when it was burned, it was

116

burned, and there is no way anybody can make a torch burn without burning up the wood." And the young man shook her roughly and pointed to the other torches piled in the corner and said, "When one torch burns down, you fool, you get another one, and you keep a torch burning all night." "Why?" asked Dzelarhons. "Why is it necessary to always keep a torch burning? Couldn't we just as easily put logs in the fire and. . . ." and the young man slapped her face and said, "You are my wife, you will do as you are told." And then he told her to go and get him something to eat.

Dzelarhons pulled on her scorched and ruined leather shirt and went outside the small house and got food for her husband. The uncle of the angry young man saw her, and saw the scorch marks on her once-beautiful shirt and the red fingermark welts on her cheek, and he hurried to the house of the angry young man and went inside and scolded his nephew. "How do you call yourself a man of our people when you treat your wife in such a fashion?" he lectured. "She is your wife and will be the mother of your children, and apart from that, you fool, her own people are not going to think much of us if they see their daughter treated so shabbily." And the uncle left the house before Dzelarhons came back with the food.

The young man was angry and insulted by what his uncle had said to him but because he dared not quarrel with his uncle, he said nothing to him. And when Dzelarhons came back, the young man took his anger out on her, and scolded her for being so slow, and called her a fool, and told her she had better learn how to do things properly or she would be very sorry.

And that night, again, he slept in the bed her

family had made, and insisted Dzelarhons hold the torch. When the torch was again burned so low it was scorching her hand, Dzelarhons again wrapped her hand in her shirt, and this time it was the shirt made of the soft bellyfur of the young otter. And when the torch burned almost out, she rose and went to the pile and got another torch, and ignited it, and, as her husband had told her to do, she kept a torch burning all night. In the morning, her beautiful robe was ruined.

Dzelarhons had no chance to sleep during the day, for her husband insisted she get food for him, and when she had done that, there were other things he insisted she do, and, still trying to be his idea of a good wife, she did as he said, even though she had not slept at all the night before, and even though she was very tired. The young man sat in front of his house watching her busy with her chores, and when he wanted a drink of water he called, "Wife, bring me water," and she went for the water.

His uncle watched for a while, then went to his nephew and sat down beside him and said, "What are you doing?" And the nephew said, "Why do you ask?" And the uncle said, "I have never seen anyone treat a wife in such a shameful way." And the nephew, who enjoyed the power he had over Dzelarhons, laughed and said, "Perhaps you will even learn something," and he said, "She is not one of us, and who can say how their women expect to be treated." And his uncle said, "She is your wife, and so is one of us." And the nephew said, "No, she is not one of us and what is more, she is not a Princess, either, but just a woman, and her family is not wealthy, as I had thought, but only fisherfolk, like ourselves, and the only thing she has inherited from her mother is that hat with the symbol on the top, and she will do as I tell her because I am her husband." And when his uncle would have tried to reason with him, the young man grew angry and went back inside his house and closed the door.

The third night was as the second night, and Dzelarhons got no sleep at all. She guarded the torch, and, as had happened both nights previous, she was forced to protect her hand with her shirt, and the shirt was again ruined.

The fourth day she was so tired her eyes felt as if sand was caught under the lids, and her movements were slow and clumsy. The young man watched her and became increasingly angry, and finally, when she stumbled and spilled some water on the bed of furs, he beat her, and the people outside heard the beating and ran for the Mother Of All, who went to the house of her grandson and opened the door without knocking and went inside and said to him, "You will stop this insanity," and said to him, "If I am told again that you have beaten a woman, I will disown you and never again call you flesh of my flesh." And the young man said "And what good has it ever done me to be your grandson anyway, for it is only your daughters and then your granddaughters who inherit anything, and I am forced to live with my uncle, and catch fish the same as if someone else was my grandmother and not you!" And the old woman said, "You are a fool, and if you are a fisherman, that was your choice, you could have been anything else you might have wanted to be." And the young man yelled at his grandmother and said, "I could never have been Queen!" And the old woman said, "You are insane, how could you have been Mother Of All when you are not a mother. But if you apply yourself and stop being so angry and foolish, you could be the chief fisherman, or you could be chief of the hunters, or you could be anything you wanted to be," but the young man just shouted and yelled and finally the grandmother, who was Queen, left the house. And the young man turned to Dzelarhons and said, "If you ever talk to me the way that old woman did, I will beat you until you cannot talk at all." At that, Dzelarhons knew this man was insane. She also knew if she tried to leave before her own people returned, this crazy would search her out and make trouble for whoever it was had given her shelter. And so, to keep the trouble at a minimum, she pretended to be very passive and she said, "I will never talk to you like that, my husband," and he nodded and again warned her. That night, again, she guarded the torch as he ordered, and her last robe was ruined, and in the morning, when the uncle saw how badly her clothes had been burned, he offered to give her his own fine garment. And she said no, and she moved about her chores wearing only her leather pants, and so it was everyone saw the marks and bruises on her body, and everyone knew the young man was insane.

That was the day her own people came back for the wedding celebration. As soon as they saw Dzelarhons, wearing only her leather pants and her hat which she had inherited from her mother, they knew the young man was not normal. "Come with us," they said, and she agreed. The young man put out his hand and grabbed her by the arm and said, "You go no place without my permission," and she laughed, and pulled her arm free and went over to where the house of the young man was, so that from it she could bring the furs that had made the bed,

and everything that she had brought to the marriage. "Don't you touch that!" the young man said, and
he tried to stop her. Dzelarhons ignored him and
gave all her things to her friends to carry back to the
dugouts, and when she had everything that was hers,
she too walked to the beach to get in the dugout and
return across the bay to the village the newcomers
were building. And the young man, cursing at her
and insulting her, tried to stop her, and he knocked
the hat from her head.

Dzelarhons stooped to pick up the hat and the
young man tried to hit her. She said a magic word
and the hat turned from woven fibre to a hard metal
that glowed with the colour of the bark of the
arbutus tree, and with one easy flick of her wrist,
she sent the hat sailing from the ground, up to hit
the young man under the chin with more force than
a blow from the fist of a powerful man. The young
man fell backwards on the sand, and lay there,
unconscious, and Dzelarhons put her hat back on
her head and, still wearing only her leather pants,
climbed into the canoe and picked up a paddle. All
her people did the same and inside no time at all,
before even the young man had time to return to his
senses, the newcomers had left and gone back to the
village they were building.

Dzelarhons went immediately to the house of her
mother, and took off her copper hat and laid it on
the floor beside her own bed, then climbed onto her
couch and fell asleep. Everyone could see the marks
on her shoulders and back, on her ribs and arms,
and they could tell from the dark circles under her
eyes and the way she slept like a stone that her time
with those other people had not been pleasant. And
while Dzelarhons slept, the men of the newcomers

talked about it and worked themselves into a fury and asked themselves what manner of people would just stand around like dead or brainless things and listen while a man abused his wife. And the more they talked, the angrier they got, and finally, they decided they were going to go back across the bay and teach some people some lessons, so that never again would GrizzlyBear people dare abuse the women of the Sea People.

When Dzelarhons wakened, she was alone in the half-built village. She did not know that all the men had gone across the bay to make war on the GrizzlyBear people, nor did she know the women and children had gone along to watch the lesson being delivered. She thought the people had abandoned her. She thought the people were so humiliated by the way the crazy young man had treated her that they had left her alone with her shame, so, confused and disoriented by beatings and lack of sleep, Dzelarhons ran from the house into the forest, leaving behind her copper hat.

The newcomers landed on the shore of the village of the GrizzlyBear people and they derided the Grizzlybear people for being cowards, and for allowing a crazy to beat a woman, and they insulted the GrizzlyBear people, even their Queen, and soon, of course, everyone was fighting, and people who should have lived to an old age, died that afternoon, and the fight might have gone on forever, except for the wisdom of two women; the Queen of the GrizzlyBear people and the mother of Dzelarhons,

"Stop!" the old queen ordered. "Stop, there has been enough of beating on people and hitting people, and shouting. Stop! Had my grandson not acted like this towards Dzelarhons we would even now be dancing and singing and celebrating together and our people would be joined as one." "Stop!" shouted the mother of Dzelarhons. "Had my daughter but run to the house of the Queen the first time the crazy man hit her she would not have been bruised and injured."

"Stop," said the fighters on both sides, "for the ones who are dead are not the culprit, and we have killed innocent people," and so the fighting stopped, finally, but many dead bodies lay on the sand. There were not enough of the GrizzlyBear people left to make a proper village, and not enough of the Salmon people left to make a separate village, and so it was that the two people decided to combine their forces and become one village and work together instead of fighting.

"Here you," the Queen called to her crazy grandson, "You wanted to be ruler, you wanted power, you wanted to give orders, you wanted to be the highest of all, well, now is your chance. We are all going to leave you here, and this village will be yours, and you can rule all those who remain here with you, and give them orders, and beat them if they do not do as you want, but for the rest of us, we are moving across the bay, for there is blood in the sand here, and the ravens of death gather in the trees, and it is no place for people any more." And they left the young crazy with the dead and took everything with them and moved across the bay. "And if you follow us," the old Queen said, "we will kill you, for you are not of us and we will not have you live with us and you are not my grandson any more," and she gave to him the deepest of insults, and it was the first time anyone had heard this insult, but they remembered it. "I do not know you," said the Queen to her crazy grandson, "and when I look where you are, I see through you. There is nothing there. I see through you," and she left and never spoke his name again.

When the people got back to the village there was no sign of Dzelarhons, only her copper hat on the floor beside her bed in her mother's house. "We must find her," they cried, "for she is sure to think we do not love her," and they began searching for her, calling her name, and asking the wind to let her know they wanted her back.

But Dzelarhons did not hear them. Deafened by grief and made half wild by loneliness and fear, she ran into the forest and headed for the mountains and finally, the people knew she was not going to return. What they did find, though, was a special place, a wonderful place, a place where a clear inland lake with fine fat trout sparkled in the sunlight. "This must be Dzelarhons' lake," they said, "for it is the most beautiful lake we have ever seen, as Dzelarhons was the most beautiful of women." And they followed the stream that fed into the lake and found at its source an enormous granite boulder. This boulder stood taller than four people standing on each other's shoulders, and there was a deep split at the bottom of the boulder, so that the stream ran as if between two legs, and from the place where the two halves became one, the water burst from the rock, gushing clear and cold, and nobody could explain the mystery of a rock that gave birth to water. "This," they said, "is a gift from the magic ones, and we will call this Dzelarhons, for this is the source of all water, as Dzelarhons is the source of our newly formed alliance," and they returned to the village and lived together.

II
_____

Dzelarhons lived behind the lake that grew from the stream that spouted from the cleft in the giant rock the people had named after her. She lived in the forest that grew up the side of the mountain, and from time to time the people caught glimpses of her. Some berrypicking women caught sight of her and called to her, "Our cousin, our cousin, come with us," but she ran from them, and some other women gathering mushrooms and fungi saw her and called, "Do not live alone, come live with us," but she had learned of the great battle between the people and blamed herself for it, and ran and hid. Some men hunting the deer heard her and called loudly, "Sister, sister, do not be afraid," but she did not know if they were men of her Salmon people or men of the GrizzlyBear people, and she hid, not knowing the two people were now one tribe. In time the people called her Mountain

Woman, or Mountain Spirit, and they often left food for her, to try to show her they still loved her and missed her.

Dzelarhons found the food, and ate it, and wept with loneliness, but she dared not break her self-imposed exile, for she still did not know the two clans had become a tribe, and she still blamed herself for the war and thought surely everyone else must blame her, too. To show her appreciation for the food, she carved frog images for the people and left them in the forest, for the people to find, and sometimes she would find or make lumps of copper, which she also left for the people, and the people learned they could flatten the copper by pounding on it with a wooden mallet, and that they could turn it into thin sheets on which they could carve figures and representations of their visions and their dreams of spirit creatures.

Alone in the forest, Dzelarhons was often sad, and she forgot how to speak any language at all. One night, as she was sitting alone in the darkness, she heard the small tree frogs singing to each other, and the sound was so pleasant to her that she tried to imitate it. At first the sound which came out of her mouth frightened the frogs into silence, but after many nights and many attempts, Dzelarhons learned to imitate the song of the frog so well she could sing with them. And the people, hearing the song, thought there was an enormous frog living in the woods, and they considered that to be magic.

Dzelarhons sang with the frogs every night, and soon they forgot she was a woman, and moved closer to her, and stared at her with their bright eyes and smiled at her with their wide smiling mouths. Dzelarhons became so accustomed to the sight of frogs' faces, and she lived so far from the people, she began to forget she was a woman, and to think of herself as a frog, and so it was when she caught sight of her own reflection in a pool of still water, she thought herself ugly, for there wasn't much to her mouth, and her smile did not stretch almost all the way around her head, and she was ashamed of her appearance. She brooded on it for days and tried to alter the way she looked. She took a piece of charcoal and drew dark lines on her mouth, to try to make it look like the mouth of a frog, but all it looked like was the mouth of a woman trying to look like a frog, and that wasn't good enough. So she patiently and carefully carved and polished a saucer of bone, and made a design on it, and into the design set small pieces of copper and small pieces of the coloured abalone shell, and when she was satisfied with the labret, she cut open her bottom lip and fitted the saucer into the slit, and though it hurt and it bled, she left it there until her lip healed around the labret and the scar held it firmly in place. Then she looked into the water and was satisfied, for she looked as much like a frog as she was ever going to be able to look, and in her opinion, she looked more beautiful than at any other time in her life.

She found, one day, a straight branch of wood around which grew a thick vine, and carefully, patiently, over a very long time, she carved at it with a sharp-edged piece of slate, separating the finger-thick vine from the bark of the branch, leaving it to wind itself free of its companion from top to bottom, and on the top, on the knotty knob handle, she carved the figure of a frog, and she decided this was her power stick, or her power wand, and that she would learn to use it properly.

And still the people heard her voice and left her gifts of food and of clothes, and she accepted the food gladly, but left the clothes untouched for she had learned that clothes, however beautiful, can be destroyed and it was clothing that had been part of the reason for the war, and so she was naked, summer and winter, warm weather and cold, and her hair grew long and hung down her back, wild and tangled.

She lived on the side of the mountain and sometimes she would find places where steam hissed from cracks in the rocks, or places where the water was so hot in the small pools that she could not put her hand in it for danger of scalding. Dzelarhons would catch fish and put them in boiling pools and then pull them out, cooked, to be eaten with her fingers, and when she had learned which of the roots and tubers were good to eat, she could cook them the same way. She had not wanted to make a fire, because of the four nights she had spent holding a burning torch and singeing her clothes and blistering her poor hands, and now that she knew about the boiling pools, she had no need of fire, for when it was bitter cold in winter, she could sleep close to the boiling water and be kept warm by the steam. And some of the pools were not boiling, but only warm, and she could sit in the warm water while the snow fell, and never be chilled or cold.

At night, at certain times, she would see the top of the mountain glowing bright red, and would feel heat, and even sometimes see fine ash drifting on the wind, and that was a puzzle to her, and a mystery, so with the help of her power wand, she toiled up the steep side of the mountain, to the very top, and looked down into one of the miracles of this earth.

The middle of the mountain was hollow, like a bowl, and in the hollow, fire raged and seethed, and the rock bubbled like boiling water. The heat from the simmering volcano was such that Dzelarhons' hair was scorched, and no longer fell straight and thick but curled up and frizzed and was only to her shoulders, and the hair on her arms and legs was burned off altogether. The hot gas coming from the volcano was unpleasant, and she backed away, croaking in wonder and discomfort, for the fire had dried her skin and she yearned to soak her body in cool water.

All the way back down the mountain she searched for cool water, but all the streams were warm, and some of them were hot, and a few of them were boiling, and the fish were all fleeing, heading for the ocean so that they not be cooked. Dzelarhons blamed herself, and thought she must surely have insulted or angered the spirit of the volcano. She felt the earth rumble under her feet and when she looked over her shoulder, she saw a finger of flame shooting from the opening at the top of the mountain, and then the earth rumbled again, and balls of fire spewed forth, setting the trees on fire.

Dzelarhons began to run, at first with fear, but then with a purpose. If the trees could catch fire, what of the houses in which lived all the people? Hadn't she caused enough trouble already? Hadn't those poor people already been visited by a war because of her, were they now to be burned to death in their houses because she had the audacity to annoy the spirit of the volcano?

And so she ran down the mountain, croaking like a frog, trying to warn the people, but of course none of the people understood the language of the frogs.

When they looked from their houses, all they could see was a beautiful glow in the night sky, and so they sat outside their houses and watched, and listened to the croaking of the giant frog.

On a hill near the ocean, in a purification hut or waiting house, a young woman who was experiencing her first menstrual period heard the frogs and though she was not allowed to leave her hut or mix with the others until her time was finished, she did manage to find a small crack in the wall and through it watch the magical glow.

This young woman's family was a family that had often left food for Dzelarhons, and in return for the food had been given many lumps of copper, which they had pounded into thin flat plates, or coppers, and on which they had inscribed the story of their family, and when this young woman had begun to prepare for her puberty time, they had banked the waiting house with these copper shields, that all who passed, though they were forbidden to enter the hut and disturb the young woman's meditation, would know that it was from their family a new woman was emerging.

Dzelarhons was still croaking a warning, and the frogs in the forest heard it and understood. They began to hop toward the ocean, where they would be safe, and the people had never before seen so many frogs moving at the same time. Some of the young people thought the frogs were bad luck, and they tried to chase them away; then, when the frogs would not go away, but rather came by greater and greater numbers, the young people began to throw the frogs into the fire, to kill them. One young person even ran into the house of Dzelarhons' mother and brought out the metal hat and used it to scoop up frogs and throw them into the flames. But the frogs came out of the fire untouched, except that the copper from the hat melted and when they came from the flames, their eyes and mouths were made of the metal, and the reflection of the flames, flickering in the copper, terrified the people, and they began to run around in terrified circles, not knowing what to do.

And from the forest came Dzelarhons, only nobody knew it was her, for her hair was completely different, and her mouth distorted by the labret, and while she thought she was calling a warning to them, they thought she was a giant frog and was cursing them for the way they had mistreated the small frogs, even throwing them into the fire and turning their eyes and mouths to metal. And the people raced in panic for the shore and the canoes waiting there.

And as they pushed off into the water, a huge fireball came from the mountain, and the earth shook and trembled, and the young woman in the waiting house began to pray and to chant, for she thought she was having a spirit vision.

The fireball landed in the middle of the village and burned everything in an instant. Not a house survived, not a dish nor a piece of clothing, not a tool, not a fish net, nothing, it was all gone.

Dzelarhons, wailing with sorrow, sat in the water and watched her people fleeing, watched their village burning, and when the fire died down, she came from the water and searched through the ashes, but there was nothing left that was made of wood, or fabric, or weaving, or anything that can be consumed by fire. All that was left were stone axe heads and stone pots and lumps of copper that had

131

once been fashioned into decorations or implements.

The waiting house in which the young woman cowered was saved from the fire by the metal shields placed around it. The sparks and embers landed on the metal and slid off, and though it was fearfully hot inside, the young woman survived. For days she stayed in this waiting house, and all she had to eat was some dried fish, and the only water she had to drink was flat and tasteless. But she endured, and when the fire was out and the earth had cooled, the young woman came from the waiting house and looked at the destruction. Not a house. Nothing. No fish racks, no food store, nothing except a pile of things fashioned out of rock and a few lumps of shapeless copper. The young woman didn't even wonder who it was had gathered all these things into one place and heaped them where she could find them. She was so weak from her days of fasting and contemplation in the waiting house, and she was so certain that everything around her was only part of her vision, that she accepted calmly things that at any other time might have sent her into a storm of weeping or hysterics.

She went back to the waiting house and got the copper shields and used them in the fashion and manner of plates, and on them piled the few things that had survived the volcano.

The young woman sat next to the last treasures of the combined Salmon and GrizzlyBear people and waited, and thought about treasure and what treasure really was, for what use is an axe without a handle, and what use a delicately carved and decorated wooden bowl if a basic thing like a fire can destroy them. And she thought of the real treasure that had survived the volcano, of the songs and dances she had learned and still knew, of the poems and the stories she had remembered. And the young woman picked up two of the shapeless lumps of melted copper and she tapped them together, and a sweet sound came from them, and she sang a song about the fire, about treasure and about being glad to be alive.

From the scorched forest, a figure emerged and moved toward her, trying to join her in song. The young woman was terrified, for she had never seen anything like this. The naked woman was smeared with soot and charcoal, her hair thick with ashes, and a wide-brimmed hat sat on her head, hiding her face down almost to her nose, obscuring her eyes. The mouth was like no mouth the young woman had ever seen, for there was a large labret stuck in the bottom lip, a labret that made the woman's face look like that of a frog, and on top of the woven wide-brimmed hat was a figure of a frog, made out of copper. All around the conical peak of this hat were other, smaller copper frogs, and in one hand the woman carried a power wand with a twisted vine growing up it, and the top of the wand was sheathed in copper. That part of the wand not covered in copper was carved with human faces, and the young woman recognized some of them, the faces of her family, and she said to the ghostly figure, "You are Dzelarhons, and I am your cousin." And Dzelarhons reached into the ashes of the village and brought out the copper hat, which was, in fact, the very hat that had been worn by the family back to the time when they still lived far across the ocean in that place where the sun goes to sleep. And she gave the hat to her cousin, who was also her sister, and she began to sing a song, and the song was the history of how the family had come across the water in search of Paradise. "Teach me, Dzelarhons," the young woman wept, "for we are the last ones here, the others have gone, and we have no idea where, or if they will ever return," and Dzelarhons continued to sing the story.

Far up coast the people living there saw the smoke and flames and felt the earth heaving under their feet and they were puzzled, but knew they had an obligation to travel and make sure the combined tribe of Salmon and GrizzlyBear people were not in any danger. A very old man and his slave, accompanied by four strong pullers, headed toward the smoke and flame in a dugout fitted with a woven sail.

Dzelarhons, still singing, showed the surviving young woman that not all the dugouts had been taken by the fleeing people; several remained and had been saved because the first fire had burned the ropes holding them to the rocks, and the dugouts had floated far enough offshore that the fire could not destroy them. The young woman swam out to them, and pushed them to shore, and into them she put the evidences of her people, the stone pots, the axe heads, the lumps of copper, and all those earth things which had survived the fire.

When the upcoast people arrived, they were shocked and saddened to see that the entire village had burned, and that of all the people who had once lived there, only two remained, one a strange wild creature who would not talk to them but who stayed always close to the forest, and the other a young woman who refused to leave without taking the few canoes with the last artifacts of her family. The old man told his slave to tie the salvaged dugouts together, and they took the young woman back with them. "Dzelarhons," the young woman begged, "come with me, that all people might know you saved my life, and all people know that surely everyone would have perished but for your warning. Come with me that we may one day find our lost relatives," but Dzelarhons shook her head no, and moved back into the scorched forest, her face still hidden by the huge woven hat she wore. The rescued young woman sat alone in one of the dugouts she had saved, and on her head she put the copper hat, the one that had been Dzelarhons', and she sang a song that told how Dzelarhons the Volcano Woman, Dzelarhons the Copper Woman, Dzelarhons the Mountain Woman had warned the people, a song that told how the Frog Woman had come from the fire to bring warning.

In the far-off village, the people welcomed the rescued young woman, and listened to her song and marvelled at the story she told them. They looked at the lumps of copper, which they had never before seen, and thought them magical, and when the young woman demonstrated how the copper could be pounded and flattened and used to mark the figures telling a story, the people were amazed and considered her very wealthy. And when they saw the copper hat, they were convinced she was magical too, but she said it was not her magic, but the magic of Dzelarhons, the Copper Woman.

She lived with the far-off people, and married one of the young men from that village, and when her first son was born, she named him after her father, the Salmon Eater, and her first daughter she named after her own mother, and to them, and to the eight other children she had in her lifetime, she gave the songs and stories of the people from across the sea, the people who had returned in search of Paradise, and she told them, these are the only true wealth any person can have, for whether everything you own is burned by fire or stolen by enemy, still, if you have your songs and your dances, if you have your stories and legends, if you have your history and the history of your foremothers and forefathers, you are rich. And she told her children, memorize these, and teach them to your children, that the courage of those we have lost is never forgotten, and be sure that you pass on the names; when you are a grandmother, give your name to a granddaughter, and when you are a grandfather, give your name to a grandson, and give to them the stories that go with the name, and that way all our children and grandchildren will have true wealth, and we will be remembered. And she told them, sing of Dzelarhons and tell her stories, and always remember the frog is not food, the frog is not clothing, the frog is not to be harmed, for it was the frogs helped warn us of the volcano, and the she-frog is our sister and the he-frog is our brother and must be respected.

And so it was the family of Dzelarhons moved in two directions, again; one group heading out to sea in search of safety, and the young woman moving to the far-off village to raise her children to honour Dzelarhons.

Dzelarhons, her face hidden by the large hat, watched the young rescued woman leave with the searchers, then moved back into the forest, blaming herself for the volcanic eruption, blaming herself for all the sorrow, fear, and destruction that happened as a result of the mountain's anger; hadn't she climbed to the top of the mountain? Hadn't she dared to look down into the private belly of the mountain? She moved, weeping, to a special place, a sacred place, and began to mourn, and to fast, and to ask forgiveness, and she sang a song she composed herself, a song asking the First Mother for aid and for understanding, for compassion and for pardon. This is not the song she sang, but it is one like it.

First Mother
Earth Mother
Giver of Life
Come to me
Hold me in your mercy
There is fear
And sorrow
There is confusion
And grief
And most of all
There is guilt

First Mother
Earth Mother
Giver of Life
Come to me
I am your daughter
I am your child
There is confusion
And repentance

First Mother
Earth Mother
Giver of Life
I have need
Oh-Ai-Yah
What have I done?

Oh-Ai-Yah
What have I caused?
First Mother
Earth Mother
Giver of Life
Come to me

And while she prayed, and fasted, and sang, and waited for help, confident it would come to her, she obeyed the rules of isolation. At no time did she touch her own body; she did not cross her legs nor fold her arms, she did not clasp her hands together, nor did she rest her head upon her arm nor her chin on her hand. If she was bitten by a mosquito, she scratched the itch with a small stick, and she did not touch her food with her hands, she used small sticks to lift it, used a flat stone to hold it, and when she had need to drink, she sipped water through the hollow of a bone. She was certain it was necessary to treat her own body with absolute respect and to not annoy it or bother it with too much casual touching, but allow it to have privacy and allow it to become open to any visit by the spirits. She removed the labret from her lip, and removed all signs of decoration or vanity, she presented herself unadorned and humble, and waited and because she did these things, and did them with the proper spirit, and did them believing with every fibre of her being that there would be help, there was help for her.

Old Woman, who moves on the fog and travels on the wind, who falls with the rain and rides the waves, Old Woman, who has never ignored the call of one who is sincere, came to Dzelarhons, and visited on her a vision and an explanation.

There was a young man in a village which no longer exists, a young man of a family which no longer exists, who was consumed by curiosity. Cleaning fish one day he noticed the webbing of small muscles that come from the fins of a fish and imbed themselves in the meat and muscle of the fish, and his curiosity was aroused. He watched fish swimming in the river, and saw how the fins and the tail are moved in certain ways to cause the fish to turn, or to remain upright, or to jump, or to hold its direction, and as he watched he thought of these small muscles he had seen and instead of accepting what anyone would have known, instead of saying, well, of course the fish move those muscles the way I move mine, and the fins are as my own arms and legs, no, this young man was curious in a most unsavory way, and he had to prove things that did not need proving. He caught a young humpback, a very little young humpback, and into the muscle tissue coming from the fin on its back he pushed a small, very sharp piece of slate. There, he said, that will cut those small muscles, and I will see if what I think is true, and he put the poor little humpback into the water again, but not where it might have been able to swim to freedom, no, he put it in a place he had fenced off, and, of course, with its balance fin damaged, the poor little humpback could hardly stay upright in the water, and had to continually compensate with its other fins. Well, said this curious young man, and what will happen if I change the fins, and he pulled the suffering little thing back out of the water and trimmed the edges of the fins and then he returned the poor creature to the water...and of course it could not swim at all properly. The sharp piece of slate in its back gave

139

constant pain, the fish was losing blood and becoming quite weak, and with its fins altered it could not move as it was supposed to and it was becoming quite disoriented, dizzy and even feeling nauseated. Well, said this curious young man, and what will happen if...and he pulled the poor half-dead creature from the water and made a deep slash in the muscle near the tail.

And the mountain began to rumble with anger. The people in this village which no longer exists were terrified and raced for safety. But the curious young man was so busy watching the dying fish he paid no attention to anything, not even to the anger of the spirits which guard creation. He crouched over the river, intent on seeing as much as he could. Brother, oh brother, wept the humpback, why did you do this? Is it not enough that you can look at me and know I am beautiful, is it not enough that myself and my people willingly give ourselves to you for food, is it not enough that our flesh has fed your children, is it not enough that we fight strong water and even white water to come every year and spawn that there always be beautiful fish for you to see and good food for you to eat? Why must you hurt me, what pleasure can you get from my agony? Is not the law clearly stated that those of us who offer ourselves as food must be killed swiftly and mercifully and always with respect, always with respect? But the young man paid no attention, and concentrated on the death throes of the poor humpback.

The mountain vomited with disgust and anger and the hot air singed the innocent trees, the boiling rock destroyed the land, and it buried the village, the river, the curious young man and the agonized fish.

The eruption also destroyed the waiting house in which a young woman was experiencing her puberty passage. Unlike the young rescued woman, this young woman was killed. The roof and the side walls of the waiting house were burned, but the front wall and back wall were covered with rock, which cooled quickly and kept the shape and form of the walls. And the young woman, too, was turned to a rock statue by the lava which engulfed her; she had been praying, and her eyes were closed, and the liquid rock spewed upon her so quickly she was still sitting upright and her features were still apparent.

When everything cooled down enough for the people to return to the ruin that had been their village, they found the waiting house and the statue of the young woman, and her mother wailed and wept with sorrow, for the young woman had done no wrong. The only other thing that was at all recognizable out of all that had been a complete village was a salmon trap, coated with rusty coloured rock, and so it was the people knew that it was because of a fish, and the mistreatment of it, that the mountain had shown her anger.

Dzelarhons considered the vision, and what it meant, and continued to pray and to fast and to treat her body with respect and dignity, and she thought often of the young woman who had died. Dzelarhons believed there was justice in creation and a reason for all things, but why should a young woman be turned to a statue because of the evil work of another? Why should an innocent life be lost because of someone else's sin.

And Old Woman moved upon the face of the sea, and though Dzelarhons was far from the sea,

141

although she was inland, near a freshwater pool, bathing four times a day and rubbing her skin with balsam and cedar, she had a vision of the movement Old Woman caused. Through the cold northern waters, moving toward that part of the earth where the sky is often bright with colour and the listening ear can even hear the colours singing, leaping from blue sea toward blue sky, a small white water creature, an all white whale with a smile on her face, free and happy, the soul of the young woman migrated in a body totally unlike the one she once had, and Dzelarhons knew then, life is never lost, and though the corporate form is shed, the energy continues, and the body of the young woman was left stuck in rock but the soul moved free in another body, a body that would travel further in a year than a human in her lifetime.

Dzelarhons was comforted by the knowledge, and almost broke her fast, almost ended her prayer, but some sort of faith moved in her and she continued four more days. And during those days she thought of the curious young man who had been buried in the lava and all trace of him erased. And though she did not, yet, have a vision about him, she knew that his energy, his soul, too, had been turned loose from its meat and bones. And she knew that soul had a choice, to learn proper respect and become healing energy, or to continue moving around as stupid energy, causing stupid actions and evil behaviour. She knew the people of the village, those few who had survived, would look on the destruction and know that a lack of respect for all creation brings eventual retribution, and the people, warned, could choose for themselves how they would behave. And some, who had not always behaved properly, would try to learn to live in harmony, and would warn their people, teach their children that all things are alive and have spirits, and are worthy of respect and consideration, and that though there is a need for food, and for shelter, and for certain things to protect us from the cold, these things can be obtained properly, with thanks, with appreciation for the giving spirit of those things which give their lives so that we are able to live. As one day we will give our lives, and our bodies will give back to creation everything we have ever used or taken.

Dzelarhons relaxed, then, and went into the freshwater pool, and bathed, scrubbing herself with balsam and hemlock, with cedar and mint, and she sat in the sunlight untangling the scorched mess that was her hair. She made herself a comb and those tangles she could not work out, she cut off with her slate knife, and she burned the hair. She collected food for herself, and ate hugely, for she had been many days eating only that which is allowed to those who are fasting. And then she slept, at peace with herself, and when she wakened, she again bathed, and rubbed her skin, combed her hair, and burned the hair she found in her comb. She replaced her labret, for she still honoured the frog, and she twisted her curly hair into small braids, hundreds of them, until they all stuck out from her head like the rays of the sun, and she decorated them with berries and polished shells and the most beautiful of feathers and whatever it was she found that she thought appropriate.

She did not yet know that in the time of her fasting and her visionquest she had become half supernatural. That was something she would learn slowly, over many adventures.

III

_____

Dzelarhons wakened one morning and had no idea where she was. She had no idea how she had arrived in this place. She had memories, but not of her voyage, and, since she had no idea why she was here, or where "here" was, she determined to try to get back to where she had been. And all she knew of that was she was trying to get to the place where the sun came up in the morning.

She sat, cold and shivering, and waited for morning. But the night in that place was long. So long she thought surely she would starve to death. All she had was some smoked fish and some fat, which she used on her skin to keep the wind and sun from chapping her face and hands. But there was no sun here, and the wind did not hurt her half as much as the pain in the empty belly, and so, from time to time, she would eat a bit of the fat, and that helped to keep her alive.

And still the night continued. Days and weeks of it, and she would most surely have perished except for a miracle. The lights and colours of the sky began to sing, and in their light, shifting constantly, crackling and snapping in the unremitting black, she saw a formation of ice and snow that did not look to her like anything that had just happened. She made her way to it, and ripped it apart, and found there frozen fish and frozen meat, and even several thick warm furs in which food had been wrapped. She put one of the pelts around her, fur side in, and was immediately warm, then she sat protected from the wind by the pile of ice and snow, and she ate of the food. She sang praise and prayers to the dancing lights and colours for helping her, and for as long as the night lasted, Dzelarhons was safe. She did not live well, but she lived, and if she did not enjoy life, she endured, and trusted, and held to her faith, and to her conviction that she would, as soon as she could, get herself to a brighter, warmer place.

After some time, when she had eaten some of the food, there was room inside the structure of blocks of ice for her to crawl inside and be safer and warmer. Safe enough and warm enough that she even managed to sleep.

She was awakened by the arrival of men dressed in furs, and when they saw her, and saw she had opened their food cache, and eaten, they were enraged. They shouted at her, but she could not understand them, nor could she make them understand her, and so she could not explain anything to them. They beat her, and tore the furs from her, and when they saw she was a woman, they made use of her. Then they tied her to their sled, which was pulled by dogs, and they took her, and the food, and the hides, with them, back to where they lived in houses made of snow and ice.

The women of these people also dressed in furs, and could no more understand what Dzelarhons was saying than the men. They looked at her and saw she was a woman like themselves, but that her hair was done in a different way. And they said to their men, "She is as we are, but not from here, and she is doubtless lost, and not a thief at all, for we are supposed to share food, and share shelter, as others have fed us when we were not at home." But the men were not convinced, and anyway there were not many women, and few children, and to get more children they needed more women And the men had enjoyed themselves, and so repeatedly they used Dzelarhons, and if she tried to fend one of them off, others would come and hold her, then take their turns with her. And so she thought of running away, and thought of it often, but it was still night, and she had no idea in which direction the sun would rise, although she always had faith that it would.

She waited. She endured. She learned from the women a few of their skills, although she was never as good at any of the work as they were. She learned from them which things are good to eat and which aren't, and she learned how to turn hides and furs into warm clothes, and how to keep the lamp burning, and some few other things.

And one day it was not as dark as it had been. The sun did not show in the sky anywhere, but it was not as dark. And Dzelarhons knew the sun was coming back, again. And she waited. She watched where it was the people stored their food, and she watched which of the dogs were savage and which were friendly, and would let her pass. And she waited.

The men were not fools. You watch her, they told their wives, you watch her, otherwise she will leave and take with her things of ours, and if she gets away, you will be punished. And so the women watched, but after many days, when all Dzelarhons did was help with those things she could do and try to learn their language, and look after the children, they relaxed their vigilance.

And one day, the sun showed her face for a few moments. You watch her, the men warned, and the women, busy at their work, nodded. Dzelarhons did not want to leave when the men were away, for then they would surely blame the women, and beat the women as they had often beaten Dzelarhons, and so she waited until a time came when the men were celebrating the return of the sun. They had gone out in their skin boats, and had hunted for and caught food, and brought it back and had a feast. They were used to dried food, and frozen food, and the taste of fresh food was so wonderful to them they ate hugely, and then they coupled with the women, and went to sleep.

That is when Dzelarhons left. She rolled one of the warm furs into the shape of a women's body, and she slid it under the body of the man who had fallen asleep on top of her, and because the fur was warm, he did not know she had left him. Dzelarhons took very few things with her, for she knew the lives of these people were hard, and that each small thing had great value, and contributed to their survival. She took some food and some fat and some small tools, and crept from the shelter of snow and ice. She tossed small bits of fat to the dogs that they neither bark nor attack her, then raced to the place where the snow people kept their skin boats.

Dzelarhons

She fled in the small boat across a body of open water, and at each of the small islands of the sea, she stopped and searched for food and for anything she might use to help herself in her flight. Island by island she went, looking always for the rising of the sun, but everything here was strange, and very quickly it became obvious the night was going to fall again. It was getting colder and colder, and she might surely have perished, except that she had faith. She prayed constantly, and determined that each thing she did, whether work, or eating, sleeping, or whatever else, would in itself be a prayer, and so it was she survived.

She remembered what she had learned from the women, and put it all to use. She saw a herd of large animals, migrating, and she remembered the stories she had heard from her own people, and she stood, still and upright, and the animals, on seeing her, halted and stared. She did not move, and the animals decided she was a strangely shaped stone, and they returned to their feeding. When they lowered their heads, she moved forward four steps and stood motionless. The animals raised their heads and looked around, and saw only the same things, including the strange shaped stone. They lowered their heads to feed and Dzelarhons moved forward four steps, then stood still. And so it went until she was standing next to the beasts. Quickly, with her sharp slate knife, she severed the tendons at the back of the animal's legs, and the animal fell to the ground. Praying and giving thanks, Dzelarhons quickly finished off the animal, that it might not know pain and fear, and then she ate some of the meat raw.

Dzelarhons had eaten much raw meat with those

northern people, but she longed for cooked meat. She prayed regularly and wished for fire, but there was not even much in the way of wood in that country, so what would she burn for fuel? Still, she prayed.

And the fire answered her prayer, for Dzelarhons, though she did not know it, was become half supernatural. And the mountain spit some flame for her, so she could smoke her meat and cook her food and stay warm.

And because of the miracle that happened there, she built a circle of rocks, with a mound of rocks in the middle, to mark the place, and in the rocks were streaks from the magic fire, streaks of reddish coloured metal, like the metal into which Dzelarhons' hat had turned when she said that magic word.

With her meat, and her few tools, and her strange hide boat, she continued her travels, using the rivers and streams rather than the sea, and whenever she needed fire, all she had to do was pray, and the mountain would send her some fire.

All this belching of fire did not go unnoticed, and some other people sent hunters out to see what was happening. They found Dzelarhons, and recognized her as a person who was at least partially supernatural, for while she looked like them, and even spoke a language very similar to theirs, her style of dress and of hair was different, and she had a labret in her lip.

They also noticed Dzelarhons was pregnant, which is not an unusual thing for a woman to be, but this pregnant woman had no man with her, and that made them think there was something very magical about her. And when they saw the lumps of copper which she had with her, they thought, at first, that it

149

was the droppings of a bear; for when a bear has been eating nothing but berries for a long time, its droppings are a dark copper colour.

They asked Dzelarhons if her child was half bear, and she laughed, for their language was enough like hers to understand, but the accent was strange, and to her, comical. And to think the child would be half bear seemed to her to be a very funny thing.

She told them her child would come soon, and they would see it was not a bear child. And she told them that it was not bear droppings she had, but a kind of rock that could be pounded into many shapes, and could be very useful, and very decorative, and because they were willing to help her, she gave them some of the metal, and showed them how to work it.

Of course they asked her where it came from, and she told them from the private belly of the mountain, and so they went together to a smoking mountain, and found copper.

They took the copper back to their people, and Dzelarhons went with them, and it was while she was with the people, she gave birth to her child. The little boy did not in any way resemble a bear, and the people laughed when they remembered their suspicions about his father. Dzelarhons told them how it was she had become pregnant, and told them that it was not the child's fault if the men who were his father had behaved as they had. "He has not lost a father," she laughed, "for every man here is his father, and will laugh with and because of him, and will enjoy playing with him and teaching him. But those others, they have lost a son, and for all their lives they will feel incomplete." And to make sure the child never knew the shameful circumstances of his conception, she forgot all about those men, and caused everyone else to forget about them too, and so it was the child grew up knowing only who his mother was, and thinking every man his father. And all the men of that area believed, as the child did, that they were all fathers to him, and even to all the other children, and that only the mother-link was special, and this re-enforced the tradition of inheriting only from the female line.

After a while the people wanted to return for more copper, and asked Dzelarhons to go with the men, to guide them. The women of that place all offered to help care for the child of Dzelarhons, and when she said she did not want him to forget her, they promised to tell him often of the story of her arrival, and of why it was she had gone for more copper.

Dzelarhons left again for the mountains, and again helped them find copper, but the men had not learned from the story of the northern men and the way they had treated Dzelarhons. They tried to become intimate with her, and when she told them to leave her alone, they ignored her, and that insulted her and made her angry. She sat down and did magic and caused molten copper and fire to surround her from the waist down, and she would not come from the burning lake, even though they begged her. They went away for a while, and talked about it, and then decided they would try to pull her from this lake. But when they got back to her, the fire and liquid rock had grown, and covered her from her breasts, with only her shoulders and head showing. "Go away," she said, "I have no trust for you, I have no faith in you, and I will not stay with you." And they apologized, for they knew they had wronged her, and knew that without her there would only be little bits of copper, and not the large amounts they wanted. But she just laughed at them, and sat in the lava, and it crept up to her chin. "Go away," she said, "or I will drown you in this hot melted rock. Go away, and if you repent of the way you treated me, then do it by showing kindness to my son, and by telling him this story. And to show you that though I neither trust you nor have faith in you, I have fondness for you because of the kindness shown me, here is some of my metal." And she gave them copper to take back with them. Then she sank under the hot rock, and they left in fear, thinking they had been the cause of her death. They expected the world to fall on them, and when it didn't, they decided it had stayed in place only because of her concern for her son, and so they treated her son very well, and told him his mother was the woman who holds the world in place, and told him his mother was the woman who keeps the mountain spirits happy. And that son was the first of the Copper tribe of the northlands.

When the men had gone, Dzelarhons came from the lava, and knew herself to be at least partly supernatural, and knew that was why the heat of the molten rock had not consumed her. She gave thanks, and sang many songs, and then started her voyage again, journeying sometimes by land and sometimes by water, and the songs she sang became songs of a certain kind. This is not one of those songs, but is of that style.

> Oh my child my only son
> Why have I had to leave you
> Oh my child my only son
> What has happened to you

Oh see my tears
my many tears
I shed them because my people are lost
Gone my mother
Gone my father
Gone my sister
Gone my brother
And I am alone, all alone
I am alone all alone

Beneath my feet
the stones are hard
On my skin
The wind is cold
In my heart
is sorrow
Because my people are lost
Gone my aunt
Gone my uncle
Gone my grandmother
Gone my grandfather
And I am all alone, all alone
I am alone, all alone

And the Voice Which Must Be Obeyed, the Voice Of All, the Voice Which Comes With A Loud Sound From The Sea heard, and took pity, and descended on Dzelarhons in the shape of a fogbank. Dzelarhons continued walking, in spite of the fog, and continued singing, in spite of her fear, and when the fog lifted, Dzelarhons was no longer in the land of the northern people, she was again on the coast, and again in a place she could recognize. She was so happy, she wept with joy, although she never gave over wondering about her son, and missing him.

Dzelarhons

Dzelarhons knew she was certainly now in great part supernatural, for she had survived too much that would otherwise have destroyed a human, and so, to reflect on her state, she went to a sweetwater pool, and made herself a shelter, and put in a supply of simple food, and again went into seclusion, dreaming and singing, sitting in a certain way, sleeping in a certain way, respecting her body, and bathing often, with cedar and hemlock, with balsam and mint. And she sang her prayers, and this is not one of the prayers she sang, but it is like hers.

> I can only have faith
> I can only accept
> I do not understand
> I do not have to
>
> I know you are there
> I know you watch over me
> I know you will come
> To help me
>
> Your time is not mine
> And so I will wait
> With my faith in my hands
> And my faith on my face
>
> There is no one here with me
> But I am not alone
> I am the only person here
> But I am not alone

The Voice From The Sea, the Loud Noise From The Sea heard this song and was pleased, and knew Dzelarhons had begun to understand many things.

And Loud Noise From The Sea blessed Dzelarhons, and put a blessing on all her children as well, for she was to have many more children, and Dzelarhons came from her seclusion house knowing she had become almost entirely supernatural.

Now it happened that a young man was out looking for food, and he came to a place where he saw fish leaving the ocean and swimming up a stream, and he made himself a trap, and caught many of the fish. He split them and gutted them, and built a rack to smoke them over a fire, and one fine fish he saved for his supper.

This young man knew of the law that required all people who take fish for food to respect them, and everything he did in the catching and preparing of the food, he did correctly. Then, when he had roasted a fish supper for himself, he sat down to eat. No sooner had he taken the fish from the fire than a frog jumped from the ferns at the edge of the forest, and hopped toward him. The young man stared at this strange thing and decided he did not like it. He did not like its large eyes, and he did not like its large mouth. So he picked it up and threw it back into the forest and told it to go away and leave him to eat his supper in peace.

The frog re-emerged from the forest, limping as it hopped, for the young man had thrown it forcefully. Again the young man picked up the frog and threw it into the bushes. The third time the frog came from the forest, the young man, angry, picked it up and heaved it in the cooking fire.

Some few minutes later, another craft arrived at the place, cousins of the young man, and he said, "See what I have caught here today. Come, join me for supper." And the young men sat at the fire with him, and they helped him eat his supper, and then roasted another fish. And, as had happened already once that day, no more was the fish cooked than a frog hopped from the forest, and moved toward them. "This is strange," the young man said, and he told them how he had tried to make an earlier frog stay away, and how, in the end, he had thrown it in the fire. The newcomers listened, and then one of them reached out, picked up the frog and threw it in the fire. "There," he laughed, "we won't even waste any time trying to convince this one to stay away," and everyone laughed.

Laughed until they heard the voice from the forest, the voice of the Wailing One, the voice that cried and moaned and sang a dirge, and asked, "Where are my children, oh my precious children, where are my children gone? Who has done this, who has done this, taken my children, oh where have they gone?"

The young men stared at each other, and the colour left their faces, and they could not even eat the fish they had cooked. And the voice wailed even more, "Oh my children, the proud ones, the haughty ones, the large ones have done this, oh my children, the powerful ones have killed you, with no thought for me, your mother, with no thought to you, my children."

The young men moved from the fire, and crept toward their dugouts, and the Wailing Woman called in a loud voice: "You, proud ones, you haughty ones, you who have no respect for the small and vulnerable, you will die, one at a time, you will die, until only the one who caused this is left, and that one will go to his village and tell this story, and warn his people, and then he, too, shall die. And if the people do not atone for what this one has done, the entire village will perish." And she began to wail again, "Oh my son, oh my daughter, oh my precious ones, what have they done to you?"

The young men raced for one dugout, and all got in, and began to pull with all their strength, and in mid-stroke, one of them fell dead. The others, terrified, pulled even harder, and a second one dropped dead. One by one, until there was only the first killer left alive in the dugout, and when the craft beached, the people of the village ran forward and saw their young men dead, and asked, "What happened, what happened?"

The young man who had killed the first frog knew that if he told the story, he would die, but he suspected if he did not tell the story, something worse than death would happen to him, so he kissed his mother goodbye, and kissed his sisters, and then told them what had happened, and no more had he finished his story, than he dropped dead.

And the people did not know what to do about this, so they sat down and began to discuss it. They thought that if they talked enough about it the Wailing Woman would forgive them, would think they were doing something to atone, and so all they did was sit and say the same few things over and over again.

Except for the mother and sister of the young man who had been the first to kill a frog and the last to die. Together, they went to the waiting house, and went inside, and began to pray, and to ask the spirit of the Weeping Woman to forgive their relative for

what he had done, and to carve a bowl in the shape
of a frog, a bowl they intended to offer to the sad
spirit.

All day and all night they prayed and worked, and
all that day and all that night the wailing continued,
over and over again, the sad croaking wail, "Oh my
children, my poor children, what have the proud
ones done to you?"

And the ones sitting and talking continued to sit
and talk and do nothing, and then the earth heaved,
and the mountain spewed, and the molten rock came
down, and all that was saved was the waiting house
in which the mother and daughter were praying.

They stayed there, and they prayed, and carved
the frog bowl, and carved a stick with a frog sitting
on top, and carved even the face of the Wailing
Woman. And because they did not know what she
looked like, and could only tell from the voice, and
the sorrow, they carved a face that is the face of all
mothers, and carved tears coming from the eyes, and
when their work of atonement was done, and they
knew the molten rock had cooled, they left the
waiting house and looked for the last time on what
had been their village. For as far as they could see
there was only a huge lake of cooling stone. No
houses, no people, no sign there had ever been
anything here but rock.

Sadly, they headed to the other end of the island,
where they knew there was a village. They prayed it,
too, had not been destroyed. And as they walked, and
wept, and prayed, they offered the carvings to the
weeping woman, but she did not show herself to
them.

For many days they walked, and then a dugout
came upon them, and in the dugout a young man,